DARLING, YOU'RE FINE

Based on a True Story

DARLING, YOU'RE FINE

Based on a True Story

By,

Cait Strit

Shoestring Book Publishing, Maine, USA

DARLING, YOU'RE FINE

Paperback

ISBN: 978-1-943974-52-8

Published by;
Shoestring Book Publishing.
Maine, USA

Layout and design by Shoestring Book Publishing

For information address;
shoestringpublishing4u@gmail.com
www.shoestringbookpublishing.com

Contents

Acknowledgements

Thank you to my mom who has always been my biggest support and constantly striving for me to do my best and live up to my full potential, without you this wouldn't have been possible. Thank you to my sister, Dippy Dooble who was always there in support of me and my dreams, you're the reason I ever loved reading or writing and i'm so thankful to you for that.

Preface

This book was based on true events that happened in my past. This is a journey through mental health and the hardships one might face with them. This book includes a relationship that was less than great and I hope it can give some comfort too those who are struggling to find the light at the end of the tunnel.

Prologue: Fate

I was always taught to look at life in whatever way I pleased. I was able to believe in whatever I'd felt was right, and never had to feel guiltily because of anyone around me, no one made me feel otherwise. As we go through life, we are placed in situations that we may have never thought we'd be in. I am a firm advocate that we go through life's motions, and we do this in order to gain experiences to become more educated people, most of us just don't treat it as so. The simplest things we stumble upon in life, teach us more about ourselves. The hardships we face, well, those are just battles we overcome, to create new and improved versions of ourselves. Reese Emery, is not a distinct human, because she's always evolving. The situations around me always affect the outcome of who I am, in any given moment.

Fate is something that is found along the way and placed around all of us by what we pronounce as *so called* "higher powers". I have nothing to disprove that argument so alternatively, I agree. Growing up in a household which didn't have much of a religious influence, I had the ability to formulate my own conclusions, and imagine ideas of what existed and didn't. I decided early on in life, a guy named God didn't live in the sky and rule over me, and all my decisions. As a child, I didn't think much of higher powers, fate, or even the future really. That was until, my future started to become the present, and the time I never thought I'd reach, caught up with me. This is when I dove into faith and realized there must be something bigger than me, carving my path and creating a road for my being.

It's important to note that *fate* isn't always attached to a *faith*, and I think that's a misconstrued factor in life. I have a faith and I truly believe that's what placed me in the situations I faced, to become a stronger version of myself. Fate isn't a coincidence and is not something to be over looked. I truly believe everything is placed in our lives for a reason. My story has all to do with a little word called *fate*.

Chapter 1

Fraudulent

It was hard to understand the thoughts that flew through other people's minds. And, for people like me, it was harder to understand the ones that raced through my own. Imagine what it was like trying to have a conversation with someone new, barely understanding my own racing thoughts, while trying to comprehend another's *normal ones*. "Nice to meet you, I'm Reese I have absolutely no direction in which this conversation could go, because my mind is an absolute pit of nothing," oh it was a mess I tell you. Though I struggled with whatever went on in my mind, not many people knew, I wasn't one to *gloat* about it. Kids tend to treat mental illness like a fad, it's disgusting; awareness and glorifying are not the same thing, that's something that needs to be distinguished. There were a select few who were aware of my private life, my parents, my older sister Haley, and my closest friend Malory. I kept it a secret for a simple reason, it wasn't the outside world's business what happened in my brain. I was in high school when the spiraling vortex of my life started to crumble, and no one in the hell hole needed to know except me. That's why it stayed between five people, and I planned on keeping it that way. Well, five people in addition to my Therapist and Psychiatrist. Until the *dark day* arrived, and my life was put on blast more than I'd like for it to have been.

It was close to the end of my senior year, I was almost out, we all were. Teachers were starting to close up lessons, get their final ideas in, and kids were ready to bust out the doors and start their summers. All the seniors were already planning their next year in college, getting ready to move on from their current existence, but not me. I always despised the idea of school, the only class I enjoyed was English. Reading was my niche and I found writing a story compelling. Everything else in the building seemed fake, high school was fraudulent. The people in it, weren't any different. We all held secrets and walked around with personas that weren't truly ours. I say *we*, because I didn't disclose my personal life either. That's something I enjoyed about English, versus the rest of the phony curriculum in the school, you knew a character and understood their lives. *You* became a part of *their* world, escaping from your own reality to build a world inside a novel. It seemed better than what was actually going on. In the real world, it was an intertwined mess of everyone's lives, mixed with lies, and people's false interpretations of who you really were, we all carried secrets and the high school walls were the safe they laid in, I couldn't wait to get out. Like the rest of the senior population, I wanted to ditch school and end that chapter of my life, but I wasn't quite ready to begin the next, and that's not how it all worked. All it means when something ends, is that there's a new beginning waiting around the corner.

Chapter 2

The Yellow Bug

June 8th, the day my life was permanently altered. That sounds slightly dramatic, but our lives were constantly altering, this experience just happened to be one to change mine. It was a Thursday and I went to school like all *normal* teens did, had my daily routine and dreaded every moment of it. I felt odd that day, some days my mood altered, and shifted without warning, the simplest of things could set my mind off in an opposite direction. This was one of those *off* days. My close friend Addison noticed it too, honestly, I couldn't explain to her what was off, because I didn't have much of an idea myself. I knew my mind was in lots of directions and I felt as if my body and my mind were disconnected, like I wasn't a human anymore, but a limp object of skin and bones. I felt hopeless and lost in the past, but this was getting to the point of total mental overdrive. (I feel it's important to note what I've been *diagnosed* with, and unlike some teens who *self-diagnose*, I was not of that bunch.) Depression and Anxiety, blah blah blah I know, we've heard it a million times but it's vital to the telling of the story. I had an abundance of things I liked to keep private, those little facts about me, were definitely some of them. It was a normal day, but I wasn't feeling normal in my own body. I was itching to leave the building.

On that day, I went to my classes, did what I was supposed to do, and then drove home. I always raced out of school, I would shoot straight for the exit across the building and wouldn't dare stop for a thing. If someone stopped to talk, I paid no attention, if someone bumped into me through the hall (or vice versa) oh well, nothing could get between me and the freedom of the outside world. I would hit the student parking lot, head straight for the front row (I always parked my car in the same spot for an easy exit) and was off. In my mind, the faster I was out of there, the better I would feel. It was hard to miss my car, it was a standout *to say the least…* It was a 1998 Volkswagen Beetle, oh and did I mention is was bright yellow? Yeah that was my life, remember how I talked about fake people, and putting up personas, my car was the perfect example. I hated Beetle's all my life, just so happens I got one as my first car. I never complained about the vehicle, it was my way of transportation, and honestly it was a big hit for the crowd around me. It was also my favorite color, so at least it had something going for it. The huge disappointment was the lack of AUX port in the car, I had keep a separate wireless Bluetooth speaker, just so I could listen to music, the radio didn't even work. I would situate myself, buckle in, and pull out of the parking spot as fast as I could, setting up my music while doing so (which was definitely a safety hazard). I listened to a ton of Eminem, Halsey, The Goo Goo Dolls, 2000's hits, modern Rap, and so much more. I listened to it all, and it calmed me when my head was a spiraling whirl wind of thoughts. My drive home was a long one considering I was in high school, 30-minute drive back home, so I had a lot of time to be alone with myself and my tunes. I enjoyed the drive home, it stabilized my brain when I was feeling all over the place.

Chapter 3

Streams of Water

I used to think that as a day progressed, I'd dismiss the thoughts that circulated in my head. That maybe a nap would help, or doing an activity: reading a book, or even just getting thoughts down on paper like, writing a story, keeping myself busy so I couldn't entertain the negativity in my mind. That day was different though, nothing I did seemed to drain my mind of anything. When I arrived home, I was alone. My parents both worked full time, so I was often alone at some point. I slept most of the time that day; the house was quiet, and I could use the rest, or so I thought. It was a breeze for me to pass out on the couch because 1. I had school, so I was awaking extremely early, and 2. I had drank two cups of coffee that day, so the caffeine crash was coming for me hard. I rarely remembered what I dreamt about, and most of the time if I did remember it'd be an absurd dream that didn't hold much value anyway, that day was no different. I hadn't remembered a blink of what I was thinking while I slept. Probably because all the thoughts that were racing and confusing my head, continued on when I fell asleep, leaving my brain unable to comprehend the outcome of it all, I'm not complaining though, I'd rather save myself the trouble of trying to pick apart the analytics of my dream. When I woke up my mom was home, but I had no desire to have human contact.

She noticed I was awake and said, "good morning my nap queen". I didn't even respond, just shifted my weight to the opposite side of the couch and pulled the blanket closer to my head. When I initially woke up, my mind was normal again, or so it seemed to be. It was like I had pushed a pause button, and everything stopped. I could never speak too soon though, things would sneak up on me like you couldn't believe. And there it was, the continuous thoughts. Repeated ideas I couldn't shake, and a feeling I wouldn't wish upon anyone. I felt sick, nauseous and dizzy, I attempted to get up and head to my room down the hall, but my eyes were fuzzy, and my brain was a mess, nothing seemed *okay*. I had checked my phone to look at the time, it was around 7:30pm on that Thursday, and I knew I had school the next day. I laid in my own bed for a little while, looking up at my ceiling fan as it spun, trying to focus on the rotation of the paddles so I didn't have to settle for what was going on in my mind, but it was too over powering.

All in an instant, it felt like there was a ton of bricks on my chest. I couldn't breathe, I was attempting to breathe in through my nose and out through my mouth, like my Therapist had told me to do when I felt over powered. It was a ton of crap in that moment though, it just made my heart race faster and my temples pulsate heavier. There were urges in my mind that were compelling me and forcing me to become someone I didn't want to be. I needed to find a solution, the best thing I could think of was a shower, maybe the steam would help calm me, the water to help soothe me and the sound of the droplets on my skin could comfort me.

I dragged myself to the bathroom and turned on the water, a shower sounded incredible and I honestly thought that I just needed time to calm down. When the steam started to billow over the curtain I stepped into the streaming water, letting it pour directly onto my head and straight onto my face. The feeling of the droplets seemed like it was just what I needed, the water started to deteriorate my makeup, the black mascara streaming down my face, the eyeliner beginning to blend in along with it. I scrubbed my face first, I needed to take off all the fake I had on. Getting down to the core is what I needed, it's what felt necessary. After that I just stood there, water pouring, body still. I couldn't continue to wash up, I had no motivation, no intentions to peruse my initial course of action. And all of a sudden, ideas I wish I could erase delved into my mind and I couldn't make them leave. I started to hold my head, squeezing as hard as I could to lower the words circling through my mind. Then tears, they started to blend with the water from the showerhead and I couldn't stop, my breathing was heavy again and I fell to the floor. Collapsed in horror, in helplessness, in need of assistance but not willing to give in. I gasped for air and begged for my mind to end its course. After a while I needed to get out, I was getting anxious, the ideas in my mind were becoming *reality* which meant they weren't just thoughts now.

I stumbled out of the shower and threw a towel on my body, half-assing the drying processes. I left my hair wet as it dangled along my back, there was no need to put it up, I was too concerned with what was in my mind, not on my head. I put on sweatpants and an oversized t-shirt to cover myself and paced around my small room trying to escape. Head pounding, and the thoughts were so intrusive they were creating a migraine. I couldn't stop speaking to myself, over and over I kept repeating, "I can't do it". Everything felt so overwhelming that I was to the point where I had lost all sense of self, Reese no longer existed, it was an image of her, not the actual representation. I reached a point where I held my breath to escape from reality, and that's when I knew I needed to go beyond myself to fix this, this wasn't something I could erase.

Chapter 4

Apple Juice

My Mom did not take stress well, she couldn't handle the pressure of it all. I feel like she pretended to be efficient in that area, but I knew that she truly couldn't stand being in a position like that. When I approached my Mom in the current state I was in, from that very moment she knew something was wrong. I was still repeating "I can't do it" like a robot and breathing so heavy that it was barely audible. My head was being crushed by my palms and I couldn't stop. Immediately she sat me down asked me what was wrong, and I couldn't respond, it was all too much. Repeating the same sentence over again and not stopping, she realized I needed to get help. After reaching out to my Psychiatrist, she got me in the car, and brought me to a local Hospital. One thing I will never forget is the amount of hysteric crying I did, followed by blank stares and empty thoughts. It was like an on/off switch, but I couldn't figure out what the trigger was or how to stop it.

Upon arrival, my Mom signed me in and we sat in the waiting room, at this point I felt like absolute nothing. The area of my mind which delivered emotion, and reason, and action, they all shut down. I sat like a painting, nothing to say, nothing to do. The thoughts were still there but my body was done fighting back, I just sat there and took it.

When they called "Reese Emery?", I entered a room where someone questioned me, she was a woman with little compassion and small understanding (from my interpretation) for those whose suffer from mental illness. It was difficult to explain the situation, and all of the details because it was still happening, and I wasn't completely aware of everything that was going on. I was lost, and confused, not much of what I said could have made much sense, which I could tell made her angry, but I couldn't help it. After attempting to explain the situation she asked me a dreaded question, one that I should've realized they would ask.

"Are you taking any medications? If so what are you prescribed and how long have you been on them, I need as much information that you are able to provide". I didn't want to answer because I could see my Mom out of the corner of my eye and I knew her reaction wouldn't be pleasant.

"I have multiple prescriptions…" I stopped short before continuing what was left on my mind. The lady questioning me was eager to speak anyway.

"Okay can you state them for me?"

"But I stopped taking them…"

She responded with, "Hmm, and what do these medications treat?"

"Well, I have Depression and Anxiety", I didn't enjoy talking to anyone about my conditions, especially those who I felt were judging me. I wasn't in a comfortable situation and I didn't want to continue further with her, she didn't seem to care at all, so why should I give in?

"Why did you stop taking them?" Then I had to go into the detail about something I hadn't fully answered *myself* yet.

"I don't really know, it didn't seem to matter much I guess." How do you explain this to someone who doesn't understand your mind at all, and all while in front of the woman who raised you, that had been there, trying to provide the best support she could, it wasn't easy to confront people with the truth, especially when you haven't come to terms with it yourself? I felt the disappointment from my Mom, and I could feel the overwhelming disapproval and misunderstanding from the women who was bartering me with all of those questions.

After the hassle of questioning and blood pressure crap, I was sent to the Psychiatric Unit. They make you leave everything you own in a locked room, they search you, and make you wear a gown and Hospital socks, so you have no ability to harm yourself or those among you. No phones allowed, no belongings at all.

A white room, plain as could be. A television built into the wall, I guess for some entertainment, but I didn't like TV and the idea of it in a Psychiatric Unit didn't make sense to me, so I never turned it on, though my Mom would have enjoyed the entertainment I couldn't handle it. There was a small, uncomfortable bed, it felt like planks of wood with a small cushion attached. There was a tiny table next to a chair that were bolted into the ground. There was a window, which I found interesting because the glass was so frosted that the point of it being there had none. It was a confusing spot for a frosted glass window but I had no room to complain, I initially put myself in this place.

My Mom stayed with me throughout most of the process. I was in the Hospital longer than expected. Usually patients were in and out fairly quick and treated or placed where they needed to be. I was held there for evaluation, to figure out what treatment I needed to be accommodated with. When my Mom did leave, it was when I was falling asleep. The staff thought I might have been evaluated during the night, they could interrupt you whenever they pleased.

A doctor came into the room very late at night, or very early in the morning, whatever perspective you see it from. I want to say around 3:30am he approached me and asked me a ton of questions. Life questions, questions about my current state, about the state I was in before being admitted, and the whole nine yards. I had initially assumed that was it, and then I could be told what needs to be done next. Boy, was I wrong. I fell back asleep in the plain white room and wondered what was happening to my world.

When I woke back up, my Mom was there. Watching television, so I assume she couldn't stand the silence any longer, it's funny because I didn't mind it, I quite enjoyed it. The peace and quiet felt like something I didn't get much in my own mind, but I knew it was a way for her to cope so, I never mentioned anything about her having it on.

The nurse brought in breakfast for me, along with my medicine to begin taking it again, it was like staring at an old friend and feeling guilty about the way things ended. I didn't want to dive right in and swallow the pills, but I knew I needed to get them in my system, especially with my Mom hovering over my shoulder. I ate my pancakes before I even began to think about actually consuming the medicine. I realized though, what am I so afraid of? The ability of recovering? That was why I was placed in the Hospital, right? To get better… so I picked up the cup of apple juice and swallowed the pills with no thoughts lingering behind.

The Hospital staff eventually came in to take my blood pressure, which was always low for some reason. When the nurse approached she informed us that the man that came in (the doctor the previous night) was there to pre-evaluate, he was a doctor, not a trained therapist; that I would be spoken to during that day, no more information was given but I knew at least I was on the waiting list for some time soon. I had three meals that day, meaning it was a long process. Lunch, was a turkey sandwich, Dinner was baked ziti (honestly it wasn't terrible).

When I was approached by a woman I hadn't seen yet, I knew it had to be my turn to be evaluated. It was not an easy process to go through, it was a lot of questions, ones I had honestly already answered to other people in the Hospital and I was fed up with being asked over and over about it all. I understood the importance of the correct information to come up with a solution, but I don't want to have to repeat a traumatic experience three separate times within a 24-hour period, who would? I was asked about everything pertaining to my life, this woman knows my entire life story, *and some.* I had to explain past episodes, my home life, my previous encounters with self-harm and all the things I had no desire to tell a stranger, but I guess needed to in order to receive help.

After the therapist spoke to me, she did with my Mom as well, privately. They went out into the hall and spoke about whatever they needed to. I guess she asked my Mom about her take on the situation, as an outsider. I guess it's helpful to have multiple opinions, especially from a parent.

When my mother entered the room with the therapist, they both sat down, my Mom on the chair, and the lady on the foot of the uncomfortable plank bed. She concluded her evaluation, that's what the look on her face meant. And the desperation in my Mom's eyes spoke volumes about what they had talked about. I didn't even need to hear the conversation they had to know it broke my Mom's heart. She only ever wanted to see me thrive, but I was stuck in a white room being evaluated by the Psychiatric Department of a Hospital. When the lady spoke she said, "What you have portrayed to me, and the actions you have shown, display that you need more than to just be sent home after talking about your thoughts, it's safe to say that if you are willing to, it is highly recommended you attended a multiple day inpatient program for mental health". It shook me to the core, I wasn't entirely sure what was going to come of having a visit to the Hospital, but I wasn't completely set on the fact I'd be sent somewhere for my behavior and mindset. I was silent for a moment then I slowly nodded in agreement. There was no denying the truth from that point, and I gathered that it must have been the best option. Everyone gets faced with things they never quite imagined, and this happened to be one of those moments.

The Hospital gathered information about the facility I would be attending, the Therapist entered with a few pieces of paper and handed them to me. I glanced over the initial paper and the first thing that stood out was the name, Overbrooke Psychiatric Facility. That was going to be my house of residence for a little while and I wasn't too sure how to put it all together. Another piece of information on the page that stood out was the age range. I realized a little further down in the text it read "Adult Facility and accommodations, 18+ personnel only". It was then I was faced with the fact I wasn't going to be in a building with a bunch of teens with mental illnesses, I would be with people of all ages, people who have experienced more than I could ever imagine and then it hit me, I was no longer a kid.

Before I left the Hospital, I asked the staff if I was allowed to use the phone to call someone. Malory must have been a little worried I didn't attend school that day, and that she hadn't heard from me in multiple hours, more than 24, which is way more than we usually went without communicating. I dialed her number and it rang about three times before she answered, she was a tad confused, until she heard my voice on the other end. She was filled with relief and I could feel the comfort through the phone. I told her a little bit about the situation and explained I hadn't much information on what was happening next, but I hoped it would improve everything. It was important to me that no one knew about the things that ran through my personal life. Malory was one of the only people that knew about my life and I liked it that way. The less people that knew about me, the less people I had to entertain about myself. She told me that if anyone asked where I was she'd say I was in the Hospital with a bad stomach bug and I wasn't allowed to have my phone. I trusted her with a lot and I rarely trusted other people. She's someone that stuck by my side whenever something happened, she actually cared. It was hard to hang up the phone, Malory was the type to brush things off when they seriously bothered her. I could tell she didn't settle right with this, but knew it was for the best, or at least I'd hoped. We said our good-byes and I hung up the phone.

When the gurney arrived with two men ready to wheel me away I was shocked that it was all coming to life. All the thoughts in my mind found a way to overtake my outside life, the ideas in my head started to affect me more than just internally. They set me up on the gurney and placed a blanket over me; I couldn't stop shivering, I couldn't tell if it was my body temperature or the nerves, either way I needed the comfort. They strapped me in pretty tight and set me up to bring me away. I glanced over to my right and saw my Mom reach over to grab my hand, she just stared at me with a hopefulness in her eyes. She hugged me tight and told me she loved me, I wasn't sure the next time I'd see her, but I hoped when I did, I would be a better form of myself than I was in that moment. She left as the medics wheeled me away, to gather some clothing and books for me to have in Overbrooke. She would bring them to me when I was there, but I wouldn't be able to see her once I was officially admitted.

I was rolled into an ambulance and one of the medics stayed in the back with me. He was a little awkward, but all I could focus on was the fact that I was in the back of an ambulance strapped down, for the first time in my life. The medic tried to carry some conversation with me, as if it would calm my nerves, but everything was happening and changing and not much could alter my state of mind. The man asked me if I was nervous sitting in an ambulance with two guys, and I honestly wasn't, until he mentioned that detail. He reassured me that I was fine, and I had nothing to worry about; the amount of times I heard that, never got rid of my anxiety before. He told me he doesn't know much about Overbrooke and the treatment there, but he understood that cooperating was the most efficient way to work the program. I took the advice and continued on my train of thought, wondering where everything was going from there. The ambulance pulled up to a building with what seemed like a never-ending entrance, the driver pulled up directly to a door that read "Overbrooke EXIT". They pulled open the ambulance doors and I felt the gust of wind hit my face. They began to unlock the gurney and bring pull me put of the vehicle. That was it. There was no backing out, no turning around. I still can't fully explain how I felt, anxious, terrified, and a tad guilty that I let this happen to myself. They pulled me out of the back of the ambulance and began to roll me in

Chapter 5

XXOO

The experience of being rolled into a Psychiatric facility from an ambulance, strapped into a gurney, is unlike any other I had before. My nerves were at a high ten and I didn't have much expectations, all my mind could compile was "am I going insane?", it was difficult to think otherwise. When the medics pulled me through the Overbrooke EXIT door there was a rough bump I had to make it over. The two things I was focused on was 1. The fact that we were entering through an exit, that was an oxymoron, and 2. The fact that the gurney had to be rolled over a bump in the pavement made me think it was ironic that I was easily pulled over a physical bump in the road, but mental ones were more difficult to overcome, those were internal. They rolled me down a hallway past a few rooms of people, I felt like a subject of test, everyone was staring at me, probably all wondering what I was being pulled in for.

We took a sharp left and turned into a corner with huge double doors. The medics didn't have a special card to enter through the huge metal doors, so they had to call in through an intercom to send for someone to open them. A man showed up, swiped his card and the doors slowly pulled open. As they pushed me passed the doors they automatically shut, they were probably on some sort of timer or sensor. As I was arriving down the hall on the gurney they stopped me at a desk with a few staff members behind it. There were patients in the same area, all looking at me, I must have looked terrified. One guy, someone I would've guessed was in his twenties smiled at me and said "Hi" but I couldn't respond verbally I was in shock, I just slightly lifted my right arm and gave him a cruddy wave back. I wasn't intending to be rude, I just had no direction for which my mind could stay in. The one awkward medic that sat in the back of the ambulance with me came over and began to lower the gurney. He unstrapped me from it and told me I could remove myself from where I was laying. Hesitantly, I picked up my head and pushed myself slowly off of the surface, standing directly next to it in my hospital gown and hospital socks; my body was still as could be with no intentions of moving.

I was pulled out of my own world when I realized a woman had been calling me to take a seat, so she could calculate my blood pressure. I apologized and made my way over to a chair set up next to a blood pressure device. She strapped my arm in and pressed a button for it to begin to squeeze tight. While this was happening she introduced herself, "My name is Mary, I am one of the staff members here, what was your name?" I sat there looking at the blood pressure band on my arm and finally glanced up to catch a glimpse of her face. Her features were soft, she had long brown hair, a tad frizzy but I understood, it was late in the night and who knows how long she must have been stuck there for. She had a delicate smile plastered across her lips and I responded with a simple answer.

"Oh, I'm Reese" I didn't have much else to say, and I wasn't sure if she was trying to receive information about my admittance of if what she was doing was an act of comfort, either way I didn't want to engage.

"It's nice to meet you sweetheart, you look a tad tense, are you okay?" I found it interesting that she asked if the state I was in was something I would refer to as *okay*, obviously if I was there, I was not perfectly fine. "Wow, your blood pressure is extremely low, you need to drink some water, walk around a little bit you've probably been stuck in one place for too long." Mary released me from the Velcro and motioned for me to stand up, I did so and she had me follow her into the room right in front of us. I approached the doorway and second-guessed walking in, there were multiple adults in there, all watching a television screen, eating snacks. It smelled vividly of popcorn, and all of a sudden Mary spoke up. "Hello everyone, I hope your evening is going well, just a reminder the Dayroom will only be open for another hour, and then its curfew for all, I would also like to take a minute to welcome our newcomer, her name is Reese." I felt like I was put on the spot, it was as if I was a new student walking into a brand-new school and the teacher was introducing me to my new classmates, I didn't like that attention. I took a short glance across the room at all of the people there, one of them offered me some popcorn, apparently it was movie night, I shook my head no politely and some other people introduced themselves and welcomed me. I guess it was nice to have them be so welcoming but all I wanted to do was go home, I felt uncomfortable, scared, and unsure of how to react to it all.

"Here's a cup of water, drink up and pace around for a little bit, get the blood flowing in your veins." I took the cup and walked around by the front desk for a little while, once I finished the water I approached the blood pressure station once more. Mary hooked me up again and began the process. "Hmm, still pretty low but a lot better than it was before, okay your set to go."

I stayed seated, not sure of what to do next. Someone else approached me while in my seat and introduced herself, "I'm going to need to bring you into your room for an examination, my name is Gladys by the way." She brought me to the first room on the left and as we entered she informed me that it would be my place of residence for the time I was there, room 23. She instructed me to remove my gown, so she could look for any marks or distinguishing factors on my body. I thought it was odd, but I assumed it was for safety reasons, and to ensure when I was leaving, I didn't obtain anything unusual during my stay.

"Why are you here?" A very abrupt question if you ask me, especially since I was already in an uncomfortable situation. Half naked in front of this woman I just met a few minutes ago and she was already asking for a synopsis on my mental issues. I gave her a shorthanded answer just to satisfy her curiosity and hopefully end the conversation.
"I basically had a mental breakdown, I don't know, my mind wasn't in the right place I guess." She took my answer and didn't bother me with anymore, which I was thankful for.

"Here are some toiletries, and some towels for your stay, this room is all yours at the moment, and there is a bathroom directly in here for your use *only*. Please note you are never allowed to fully close the door to your room, if you need to get changed, do so in the bathroom. You may position the door to your comfortability but always make sure someone can peek through."

I took the tray of things as she handed them to me and set them on the desk, I thanked her and as she exited the room she told me she would bring in my stuff that was verified for usage during my stay. That meant my mom had dropped off my belongings, and they had to look through them before they were promptly given to me.

When she arrived back in my room she placed a large brown paper bag on the floor with my things, she went over the list of my items and told me that all of the things I was *not* allowed to have and informed me they would be put in a locker down the hall and given back to me before my departure. She exited my room for the last time and I was finally alone. Just me in room 23, with a brown paper bag of few of my belongings and a bed to sleep in. I began to unpack my items and set them in drawers and on shelves. I organized everything as I would if I was at home, not that this was anything like being at my house, but I was attempting to make myself feel more comfortable. I pulled out all of my clothes, set them nicely in drawers and organized my journals and books on the desk provided. I left out a pair of sweat pants and a sweatshirt to wear for bed, I couldn't wait to put on real clothes again. In a hospital gown I felt so raw, so vulnerable, it's hard to explain. After I got dressed I walked over to the desk where I separated my books, I had my mom supply me with my two journals and a couple of novels: *"Invisible Man"* and *"The Alchemist"*. I wasn't allowed to use my own writing utensils, but we were allowed to use these weird rubber pens, I assume so no harm could be done. When I picked up the journal I set on top of everything else I noticed a sticky note peeking out of the side. I hadn't remembered placing any sticky notes in my journal, so I was slightly confused.

When I opened up the cover I revealed notes that were left for me. They read "I love you so much! Be strong and worry about you, nothing else. You are so beautiful and talented and have so much to offer to the people who love you, but also to the world around you. I just wish you could see what I see. I will miss you every minute, and you will be with me in my heart until I can see your beautiful face again, in hopefully a few days! Mommy loves you xxoo." That was written across four sticky notes, I chose the bed farthest from the door up against the wall (there were 2 beds, the rooms were meant for two people I assumed) and placed the notes directly next to the bed. That way, every night I would lay down I could think about my mom and what I was striving to go back to. I shut off the lights to the room and got myself into the bed. Looking up at the notes on the wall, I drifted off to sleep.

Chapter 6

Billy's Story

"RISE AND SHINE EVERYONE, TIME FOR MORNING MEDS."

Have I mentioned I am a *very* light sleeper? Some bald guy pulled my door wide open and pushed back the curtains right next to my bed, reveling the overbearing sunlight. I squinted my eyes and rolled around to the opposite side, away from with the window. Not wanting to get out of bed, he walked over to me and said, "MORNING MEDS" and that surly sent a wakeup call surging through my body. He walked out, leaving the door wide open for me to receive all the noise outside of the room. I started to remove myself from bed and searched for the socks I kicked off while I was peacefully sleeping. I situated them onto my body and hopped out of bed. The only shoes we were allowed to have were ones without laces, I had my mom pack my slip-on checkered Vans. I slid those on and started to head for the bathroom.

I glanced at myself in the mirror and I looked like a wreck, I was not used to wearing no makeup around other people, it was a different experience for me. I brushed my teeth with the supplies Overbrooke provided and washed my mouth out with some tap water. My hair was looking ratty, so I quickly placed them in two braids, as if anyone cared what I looked like, but I felt uncomfortable as it was.

I walked out into the main hall and saw a crowd of patients. There were a few lines: a line for the blood pressure, for 6:30am medicine, and the smallest line for a lady who was taking blood. I was truly hoping I wouldn't have to give any blood but surly enough, they called my name to be in the line. I always dreaded having my blood taken. After they finished sucking the blood out of me I turned to the line of medicine, the nurse had two cups laid out for each of us, one filled with water, one she filled with our daily medicine. She gave me quite a few vitamins, something that was apparently given to everyone there, and informed me to stop back at 8:00am to receive my other dose of medicine.

After all of that was said and done I returned back to room 23, unsure of what to do with myself. I didn't want to enter the Dayroom with the rest of the patients, it felt too new still. A few moments later, that bald guy came walking around the hall again, screaming "BREAKFAST IS ARRIVING NOW" so I assumed that was my cue to enter the Dayroom with everyone else.

I walked over to the line of guests and the bald man was pulling out specific trays for each of us, he called my name and I approached as he handed me my food, when I entered the room there weren't many people seated yet, most of them were waiting for their food. I was nervous I would be taking someone's seat, but then I realized I wasn't at a high school lunch table. I took a seat and opened up the tray of food. Surprisingly, the food seemed edible, there were 2 waffles, a cup of fruit, a thing of apple juice, and what I assume was oatmeal. I didn't have an appetite for the oatmeal, so I steered clear of that, but I ate the rest and actually enjoyed it. There was also 24-hour coffee privileges and extra snacks and food in the cabinets and fridge provided. I stood up and got myself a cup of coffee; it felt nice to have warm coffee linger down my throat. Coffee was a true addiction of mine, I was glad I could have it while in the facility. When I sat back down there was a guy sitting next to me. The one who had smiled a me the night before and said "Hi" to me while I was being pulled in through the doors. Turns out he was the second youngest there 28 years old, would have never guessed honestly, he seemed way younger.

I took a few sips of my coffee and he engaged in some conversation with me. I bet he could tell I felt awkward being the "*new kid*". He was a scrawny guy, scruffy brown hair, he wore glasses, and he was wearing a camo sweatshirt. He looked like the type of guy who definitely hunted animals for fun, and he seemed to belong in the South, not New Jersey. He told me his name was Billy and that he had been there for quite a while, longer than most people stay, so he understood how I was feeling and what it was like to go through the process there.

Billy's story was messed up. He opened up to me pretty quick, I guess to show that it was okay to talk to other people there, and that no one was there to judge. He told me that his girlfriend of multiple years ran off with his younger brother to start a life together, apparently, they had been "fooling around". Finding all of that out, basically made him go off the deep end. He started to drink an insane amount again and finally realized that wasn't the way he wanted to move forward. He told me he needed to face the true problems at hand a more effective way, rather than dealing with them *his* way.

I was about to tell him a little bit about myself, but some lady walked in and called my name, "Reese Emery? Hi, I'm going to be your social worker, I need to go over a few things with you."
So, I was never able to tell him why I was there, honestly it was a little bit of a relief that I didn't need to explain my story to him, its nerve racking putting yourself out there, so raw.

Chapter 7

Connect the Dots

That was my call to leave the Dayroom, so I placed my coffee on the table and started to remove myself from the seat. The Social Worker motioned for me to follow her. We entered a room past the front desk, a little further down the hall. It was a tight space, one large desk with a swivel chair for the Social Worker's comfort and two plastic chairs placed directly in front.

"This is my little office, you can have a seat in either of those chairs." I took a seat and waited as she shuffled through a file with a stack of papers. "Oh, I forgot to introduce myself I'm sorry, I'm Carol, and I will be in charge of you during your stay here. If anything isn't right, you come to me. I will be the one discussing the process with you and evaluating the end, meaning where you will continue on from this facility. Do you understand?" I nodded my head yes, she seemed like a very understanding person, probably the most compassionate staff member I had encountered, but honestly that frightened me. I didn't want to feel comfortable in this place, I thought that if I started to feel okay there, that would mean that was where I actually belonged. "Okay great, before I can release you I just need to go over a few documents with you and have you sign them and talk a little bit about yourself."

I shifted my weight to place myself more comfortably in the chair and she pushed a few documents my way. She informed me about the facility, told me more rules that I needed to obey, and explained the process there. She had me flip through the papers as she explained them, and I had to sign as she went. There seemed to have been 30 pages of instructions and dotted lines to sign. As she was finishing up, she organized the papers back into a file and pulled out a separate sheet.

"We are officially done with all of the signing, I just need you to go over a little bit about yourself." The dreaded part, the aspect of this stay that I knew would approach sooner or later, but I hoped I would've been able to prepare for it more. Although, preparing for an evaluation seems to be fake, like if you prepare, you think of what you'll say, it loses the raw emotion. I guess it was a good thing I was a tad blindsided, I just didn't want to go through the process at all.

"Whenever you're ready, I'd like for you to start explaining to me why you think you were placed here." I found it interesting that she used the words, *why you think* you were placed here. Most people referred to it as, *why are you here?* She made it seem as though it wasn't fully my fault that I was there, and I respected that. I had been feeling guilty about my new residence, pondering the idea that I put myself there and I could've fixed it before it got to that point. In that moment though, she made me realize, it wasn't *me* who got me into this mess, it was a piece of my dysfunctional mind. I took a moment to think about it all, gather my thoughts, I didn't know which direction to start in, and I always felt awkward speaking about myself (especially in that type of setting).

"Sorry it's taking me so long to respond, I just don't have much of an idea of where to even start." I took a moment to try and gather myself a little, but it didn't help. "I feel like so much has happened in the course of these past few days, that my mind is just kind of all over the place."

"Reese, don't feel ashamed, I can tell you aren't ready to open up, but there will never be a better time, it's always going to be scary, you just have to do it and all will fall into place afterward." I knew she was right, I never felt okay speaking to people about my mind, the only person I was actually comfortable with was my Therapist Ashly. But then I realized that there was even a time when her and I didn't have that connection, when I had no desire to open up. I knew that once I opened up to my Social Worker, she wouldn't judge me or anything harsh, I was more nervous of what I would think of myself afterward.

"I don't really know where to start…" I took a pause and attempted to think of what to say. "I guess I just had a lot of things cluttering my mind, I don't think my brain could handle it all, so it went into overdrive." I started to feel like I wanted to open up, but I honestly didn't know why I ended up there, I was still figuring that out. "I guess I should start off with telling you I was on medication before coming here, I had been on them for quite a while, maybe six months or so. And then one day I forgot to take a dose, then one day turned into two, and so on. And after the medicine left my system completely I guess I just became who I was previous to taking it. I didn't see much of a point of taking them. My mind was cluttered and the ideas in my brain were overwhelming enough for me to stop caring about what happened to me next. I honestly think I lost all hope for the future and saw no point in attempting to help myself. I saw no point in anything anymore. I was in a vortex of dark thoughts and I didn't have the motivation to get myself out. My negative thoughts began to consume my life, and I didn't care." I amazed myself with how much I spilled. I didn't know I had it in me, I had no idea where the courage came from to open up. I might have been holding that in for so long that I needed to let it escape.

"That's a very powerful factor, abruptly stopping medicine can drastically alter your behavior and mood, is there more behind it than that?" I knew what she was getting at, she assumed that something in my life was pressuring me to not want to take the medicine any longer. That destroying myself would mean I didn't have to focus on the real problems around me. In reality though, it just ended up consuming me.

"I guess there might have been things in my personal life that were helping me not want to take my meds."

"What were those aspects of your life?" Carol was not taking the short answer, she wanted, and I guess needed the full truth to understand where I was at.

"I mean my home life isn't amazing." I feel like this was the only part of my life that wasn't a full secret. Most people in or around my life knew I had zero connection with my father. That we didn't get along, no one knew the reasons why, they just knew I despised him.

"Tell me a little bit about that, what do you mean?"

"My father and I do not get along, I have zero interest in being around him." I wasn't ready to spill my whole life out in front of this lady, so I was trying to give her an answer without giving away full-blown details.

"And why was that?" I wasn't going to tell her all about my life so I gave her a vague answer, so we could move on.

"He's really mean and angry all the time, it's like he puts up a front. And he lies constantly, fabricates things. He drinks a lot, I guess that's why." And she left it at that, I assume she didn't need a full story, but just the gist of what went on at home. I'm sure everyone reading is wondering more about him though.

My father was a story in it of itself. Ever since I was young, we never got along, I always knew that there was something off about him, something that didn't click right with me. As I got older I began to place my thoughts about him together, I started to connect the dots. I can vividly remember waking up in the middle of the night, probably as late as 2:00am to the screaming and fighting and random items being smashed all over the floor in the kitchen. This all dates back to when I was about 4 or 5 years old. I presume it happened before I reached those ages too, I was just too young to remember those certain incidences. My parents would go at each other's throats, leaving me no other choice but to truly believe that they never belonged together. I would sneak into my older sister's room and sleep with her most nights. She would comfort me and hold my ears when the screaming became unbearable.

As I grew older I started to realize the constant bottles of liquor spanning the recycling bin.

I realized how every night my parents would come home they would have bought a handle of vodka to consume; they would go through them like water. When I could understand the concept of being an alcoholic, that's when I noticed I would never have a connection with my Father. Truly though, I didn't mind not having a relationship with him. He said the most horrid things I have ever experienced, and to the woman he was supposed to be madly in love with.

As years passed, everything only became worse. The drinking never ended, the fights never came to a halt and I seemed to be the only one who wanted to notice there was an issue. I was always on my Mother's side. But when I would argue with my Father because his drunkenness couldn't formulate actual thoughts I would bring up that I hate everything about him.

My Mom always sided with him though. I was always told to stop stirring the pot, and to leave it be. She liked to call herself the *middle man* to keep the peace, but she was just hiding the truth that she didn't want to acknowledge. That became a huge toll on my life, I was always pushed to the side, told to shut up about what was truly going on, because no one wanted to face the facts but me.

I would wish at 11:11 every day that they would split up, that I could have a happy life with just my Mom and my sister Haley. That never came true though, they continued to carry on their miserable lives together, and dragging me along with it. My Father was someone I had lost all hope for. I had no intentions of connecting with him, and I didn't want the opportunity. I hated all of the remarks he made under his breath, and all of the vulgar talk he would express to himself, thinking no one could hear. I had senses like no one else in the house, and I heard it all. I always despised hearing all of it, but it only made me realize that some people have no compassion.

I hated my Father, hate is a strong word they say, but that's the exact reason why I use it to describe how I felt toward him, there was no other explanation.

"Is there anything else you would like for me to include?" I was over talking about it all, and I was getting frustrated just thinking about my Father, I didn't have much else to say anyway.

"No that's about it" I had a feeling she wanted to know more, but she could sense my hesitance with wanting to go further.

"Okay Reese, thank you for your time, I know this isn't easy. Make sure you attend the groups and follow all the rules. You are free to go." I found it interesting she expressed I was free to go, because I wasn't, I was free from her small box of an office, but I wasn't free of this place, and most of all I was not free from all the thoughts in my mind.

Chapter 8

Everything will be Okay

Now my mind was all askew. Thoughts I didn't want to resurface had come to sit front row. Ashly was able to get me to speak, open up about myself and what was going on. It didn't make me feel any better though. I lasted so long keeping everything hidden in my mind that it was a foreign letting some of it escape.

Now my mind was stuck in the realm of my Father. A man I never felt compassion toward, a man I never wanted to build a relationship with. I kept all of the in-depth details about him in my mind, not wanting Ashly to know the full truth. I felt they were too personal, displayed too much about me and my life. I'm sure she could tell I wasn't disclosing all of the information, but I didn't mind, she initially received what she needed.

Leaving her office, I headed toward room 23, I couldn't face the Dayroom quite yet, I needed some alone time to gather myself. I positioned the door so that there was a small peek hole available, but so it was closed enough to where it felt I was in my own space.

I took a seat on the bed closest to the window and stared straight ahead at the dresser in front of me. I laid back on the bed, letting my legs flop off the edge, and I looked up at the white popcorn ceiling. I remembered the notes I had plastered on the wall, the ones from my mom. I turned to my right and curled up into the perfect position, reading the words my Mom left behind for me. I reread them over and over until my eyes didn't want to stay open any longer.

I guess I fell asleep for a little while, I was awoken by the bald man entering my room and telling me I needed to receive my 8:00am medicine.

I arrived at the medicine counter and the nurse gave me my dose of medicine. I realized I needed to attend groups to gain a sufficient stay here, so I entered the Dayroom and waited for the next meeting to start. While I was waiting I kept myself busy with coloring pages and word searches. There were multiple activity sheets of paper on the table, and I knew that would kill some time and keep me entertained. I stayed quiet and minded my own business. I picked a page with a drawing of the sun and crescent moon, with a quote that read *"Everything will be okay"*. It was a corny saying but it was the most interesting coloring page of them all.

When more patients started to filter into the room, I assumed that a group would be beginning soon. People started to fill in the seats around me and I had to start clearing the mess I had made with coloring utensils. I condensed the area of space I was taking up, but I continued to color.

Then one of the staff members entered the room and took a seat at the head of the table. It was Mary, the one I had met the previous day while she was observing my drastically low blood pressure. She began the group by introducing herself and explaining the topic of the group. It was a group about our goals for the day, ones we could *actually* accomplish.

As she went around the room asking each person what their goal was for the day, I had to think of a goal as well. The group went a little like this: *"I want to be happier"*, *"I hope to clear my mind of negativity"*, *"See the future in a positive way"*, *"To stay positive"* and about five more answers afterward.

I was nervous for the circle to catch up to me, I didn't plan on having a goal for the day, and I didn't want to repeat someone else's, that seemed phony. When it finally got around to me, I stood silent for a moment then looked down at the paper in front of me. I read the little phrase above the picture of the moon and sun.
I spoke lightly to the group around me "my goal is to convince myself everything will be okay".

I knew it sounded absurd when I spoke it out loud, but people around me seemed to enjoy the answer. I didn't even believe myself, but I felt like all the answers in the group were fake, so I didn't mind. I didn't know of anyone who would actually focus on the things they stated they would. I wanted to believe everything would turn out okay, that I didn't have to worry about the future, but I knew that was not the case.

I was the last one to share in the group, I assumed Mary went in order of the people who were admitted because Billy spoke first, and I spoke last. After we all shared our thoughts she moved on to the next topic of the meeting, warning signs and triggers.

She talked about the topic and we all sat there and listened. I faded into my own world at some points, not even realizing I wasn't paying attention.

When the group was over I just continued coloring, not leaving my spot, I was content where I was.

And the rest of my first day was utterly uneventful. It was just a planned day, and we all listened to the rules and stayed on schedule, so we could get out as soon as we could. After the first meeting, there was another scheduled 30 minutes later. I came to find out, the meetings were never ending. After one, there was another. If there wasn't a meeting going on for a long period of time, it was because we were eating a meal.

Lunch was consumed at 11:00am and there were meetings sprawled out afterward. Then it was dinner at 6:00pm, and two more scheduled meetings after. The day basically ended when the last group meeting was over, it began at 8:00pm and was about 45 minutes long. I was very glad when 8:45pm hit, that meant the day was basically over and I accomplished my first day at Overbrooke.
The meetings were helpful for getting to know the other patients and receiving some advice across the board, but I was honestly ecstatic when it was done with.

I brought my coloring page back to room 23 and set it on the desk for me to finish the next day. I decided to call it a night, there was nothing left for me to do, there wasn't much for anyone to do. I turned off the lights in the room and took my place in bed. Hoping the next day would feel a little better than that day had. I still felt out of place, and I didn't know how to shake the feeling. The idea that everyone was so much older than me made me feel like my problems were inadequate compared to theirs, or at least that's what I felt they thought. Heck, I was 18 and the youngest beside me was 28, so there was already a 10-year age gap between us, imagine me compared to the rest of the population.

That was the last thing I was focused on before I fell into a deep sleep.

Chapter 9

Fogged Up

June 10th, another day waking up at 6:30am to receive morning meds. My second day at the facility had approached, and for some reason when I woke up I was convinced everything that had happened the past few days were all a dream.

Sadly, that wasn't the case.

When I rolled out of bed and removed the covers from myself, I again, found my socks, and placed my shoes on. I received my medicine and returned back to room 23 to take a shower. I felt like I hadn't washed up in a week, which wasn't the truth, it had been about two days, either way I needed a shower.

Entering the bathroom, I shut the door behind me and turned on the stream of water. It was a weak flow, but it was what I had to work with. While I was waiting for my shower to warm up I realized the last shower I had was the one I tried to clear my wind with. The memory was coming back strong and forceful, filling my mind with flashbacks of June 8th, a day I didn't want to remember.

Once the water was warm enough I entered the shower and took a deep breath, releasing all the anxiety I had toward my previous experience with streaming water. I realized the only things they provided to wash myself was a tiny towel, and a miniature sized shampoo/body wash. I didn't have anything else to use so I had to deal with what I had been given. I took my time in the shower. Letting the warmth comfort, me, although the water pressure was terrible it felt nice to have a space all for myself, where no one could bother me. I then realized this was the only place in all of Overbrooke that could give me peace and quiet.

When I exited I toweled off my body and wrapped my hair in the same one provided. Looking at myself in the mirror I noticed my features were barely visible, fogged like my mind had been the day I was brought to the Hospital.

Chapter 10

Face to Face

.

With not many fashionable options in the facility I decided to throw my hair into two braids again, put on a pair of leggings, a different sweat shirt this time, and of course the same checkered slip-on shoes with no laces. I assumed it was just about time for breakfast when I was finished with my shower, so I headed to the Dayroom to wait for my food.

When I was entering though, something made me stop for a moment. *Someone* made me stop for a moment.

I hadn't seen this particular guy the previous day, so he had to be new, he seemed unaware and absolutely dreadful. Like he had no intention of being there. As I was standing in the doorway thinking about this guy, I heard *Reese* being called for a tray of food. I made a sharp turn to grab it and entered the room after. I took a seat at the table and removed the lid off the tray. I grabbed the syrup for the waffles I was given and began to pour it into the waffles hallow pockets. When I went to reach for coffee that wasn't actually there, I realized I hadn't grabbed my morning dose yet. I pushed my chair back with a scratch on the floor and made my way toward the coffee machine, filled a cup up and doused it in cream and multiple packs of sugar. Making my way back to my seat I caught a glimpse of the new guy at the other end of the table.

I focused on his behavior, how he picked at his cuticles and wouldn't look up from his hands. I was waiting and listening closely to the names being called, trying to catch his.

"Bryce" The new guy's eyes were removed from his hands, I finally got to see his full face and noticed he had striking brown eyes. He started to pick himself up from his chair to make his way over to *his* tray of waffles.

He came back to his seat and examined the food, picking at the home fries on the side of the plate. The home fries were the best part of the tray, so I always saved them for last. While reaching for his orange juice, he seemed to be confused about the piece of paper on the edge of the tray. It listed a bunch of options of food, it was what we were allowed to choose from the day before as our meals. But, he wouldn't have known that because he wasn't here the previous day.

The entire time breakfast was happening people conversed and watched television, but no one interacted with Bryce, I knew how it felt to be new, I was still basically in the same stage as him.

I decided to help him out, "do you need help with that paper?"

He looked up at me and seemed a tad confused, maybe unsure if I was talking to him, but I guess he caught on because he replied, "Uh, yeah".
I made my way over to the opposite side of the table, picked up a rubber pen and removed the paper from his hand. I placed the paper back on the table and I began to show him how you can circle what items you want, and how you could write how many you desired. Basically, explaining that it was super easy to do, I also informed him to make sure he signed his name at the bottom when he was finished.

After I helped him, I returned back to my seat.
"Thank you."
I glanced back at Bryce and told him it was no big deal.
I just wanted him to feel welcome, like I did when I first arrived, not many people seemed interested in getting to know him.
Then he asked me a question I didn't expect, "Hey, can I... take that seat next to you, would ya mind?" I didn't mind, so I motioned for him to take a seat. He seemed thankful to have someone just to sit next to, it felt nice to help someone else. We began to talk a little, got to know each other. That's initially where our *friendship* began.

We spent most of our time in the Dayroom together. Bryce kept me entertained with stories about his outside life. We talked about a lot actually. After a little bit of warming up to each other, he *began* to tell me why he was there.

He started off by apologizing to me, which left me utterly confused. "I'm honestly sorry for last night, if I woke you, or disturbed you." I had not the slightest idea what he was talking about. I looked at him in confusion and replied;

"You didn't wake me, I didn't know who you were till this morning, I don't know what you're referring to" and I let out a small laugh, in discomfort (I tend to laugh in awkward situations).
"Oh, just uh assumed everyone heard, that's why everyone has an eye out for me, you're the only person that's been friendly."
I replied, "Well what happened, what am I missing here?"

"Right, well I came in last night still in *delusion* I guess, still had alcohol in my system and they put me here." He took a pause and seemed to be getting angrier as he spoke about the subject. "I shouldn't be here, no offense to you, or anyone here but I should be in rehab, detoxing -getting better- I mean, they detox me here, but it's not a rehab, it's a Mental Hospital."

I could tell he was not ecstatic about his placement here. Honestly, I hadn't had much to say, I was unsure of how to reply to that. I wasn't offended by the *Mental Hospital* remark, even though I bet he thought it would come off that way. That's exactly what Overbrooke was, a Mental facility. It was there to treat patients who suffer from deep lying emotions they cannot seem to cope with on their own. These are people that have hit their breaking point. I never told him this but, he must have been at that point to have been placed here.

"I'm sorry" The simplest thing I could've said, I did. I *was* sorry, in a way. I felt sorry that he was so angry to be in a place he didn't want to be, but I doubt anyone in Overbrooke said, *"Hey let's take a vacation to a Mental facility"* no one expected to be in the position they were. But to be put here, is a long process, you have to say some pretty scary shit, I guess he fit the criteria.

"It's whatever, just needa apologize to everyone I've disturbed and disrespected." I was surprised I didn't witness what happened the previous night, I was right by the main entrance and I'm not a heavy sleeper. Maybe it was those sleeping meds they put me on to regulate my sleeping pattern. "I'm not a nice person when I'm drunk, I'm glad you didn't hear it." I smiled at him kindly, to show him comfort, to let him know he wasn't alone. But I'm glad I didn't hear him lash out, it would have put me into a panicked state.

I know what it's like to deal with obliterated people, people who drink till they slur their words, they repeat themselves a hundred times, and lash out without warning. I wasn't up to sitting through another episode of it here.

"I hope you're feeling a little better now" I said to break the silence.

"I mean the alcohol's leavin' my system so I feel like crap, detoxing is a difficult road, involves not wanting to eat, shaking, headaches, major sugar cravings." I've never met someone who was actively trying to improve their drinking habits, so all of that was news to me. "But, mood's better than before, I mean not slamming doors and screaming at people. I'm calmer now. Anxious, but at least I'm talking like a normal human."
Bryce had this unique quality to his voice. It sounded *almost* southern, but he was from New Jersey, around the same area as me. He didn't seem dumb or incompetent, but maybe he was never great in school, or English. I hadn't much of an idea where his *twang* came from, but it didn't bother me. I kind of enjoyed it. It was different from most people, and it added to his character.

"That's good to hear, things get easier here I guess, the first day is awkward but people start to warm up," I had no idea how the other patients were going to interact with him, I didn't know if they witnessed him the night before, but I was trying to comfort him, to make him feel a little better. I attempted to say something to make him feel less anxious… "I thought I was going to a younger unit but they said I was too old and stuck me here, so I'm not where I expected either, it's a little weird being with people so much older than I am."
He looked over at me, "How old are ya?"

"I'm 18, I don't know why I didn't associate that with adult status, but I don't feel like I was an adult I guess, everyone there were *actual adults*."

"I ain't too old though, 26" he was right actually, he wasn't too old, most people here were in their 40's or 50's so he was young compared to most patients there. He could now be pronounced as the second youngest, next to me obviously.

"Yeah, you're one of the youngest here then, it's just odd being the youngest. It seems like everyone feels as if I haven't experienced enough to have the privilege to be here." Sure, maybe I haven't been through the same problems they have been faced with, maybe I didn't struggle with an addiction, like majority of the patients have. The glares they would send to me in the groups were assuring enough that some felt I didn't deserve to be in the same unit as them. Truth of the matter is though, we all were placed there because of a suffering with mental illness, not primarily addiction. I got just as much out of the groups as they did; I was young, but I sure as hell was not censored growing up, I was not naïve about the world and happenings around me. I knew more than I believe they realized, but I kept to myself, let them entertain their own thoughts however they pleased.

Bryce had got up to fill his coffee cup and offered to fill me one as well. I stayed seated in the same chair I had been in for quite a while, we had been talking and not paying attention to much around us. When he sat back down he brought me over a few creamers and some sugar packets, which I didn't ask for, but I guess he observed the fact that I drowned my coffee in cream and sugar the previous times I got up to refill my coffee supply.

As I was perfecting my masterpiece he sipped his coffee black. I will never understand how people can enjoy straight black coffee, it is completely baffling to me.

He glanced over at me as I was pouring in my last packet of sugar, "Darlin'? Why're here?"

It caught me off guard. To be honest he and I hadn't had much deep conversation yet. I asked him childish things like what his favorite color was, which was blue. And what kind of job he had, he worked at a

Marina. Things like, where we grew up (that's how we figured out he used to live in the same town as I did). Just small talk, to keep things light hearted in this place. For some odd reason, I felt comfortable with him, maybe it was because he didn't jump straight into asking how I ended up here, we got to know about each other first, we actually bonded and became sort of like *friends*.

I was silent for too long. I could tell he felt wrong for asking, "Uh I didn't mean a thing by that, just tryin' to talk, you don't have to tell me" I was about to respond and tell him it was okay to not feel bad about asking, but I didn't have time. "Here I'll tell you why I ended up here." He told me vaguely why he was here previously, I knew he drank but that was about it. "I've been a tad messy most my life, delinquent, got involved with drugs, sold those drugs, ran into some trouble with the law, went away for a little, and when I got back, my life got even shittier, couldn't handle the outside world on my own." I already knew before he continued, that he meant when he was released from jail, he became dependent on alcohol. "I didn't have no one to turn to, I was freshly 19 and started drinkin. Then it uh, changed my life." My heart was dropping with every word spoke. This wasn't a man that wanted his life ruined, this was a kid that was lost, and wasn't able to find the clear path after being sent away. For some reason, it hurt to hear what he was telling me.

"The reason I'm here is cause I'm a drunk, this past Tuesday I got *another* DWI, needless to say it didn't stop me from drinkin', I got really bad apparently and was taken to a Hospital. The fucked-up part isn't that I drank after a DWI, or that it wasn't my first, it was that the person who brought me to the Hospital told the people there that I was a danger to myself, that I was gonna hurt myself, that's why they messed up and put me here. I'm supposed to be in a Rehab, not a psych-ward. I haven't ever had thoughts to hurt myself I just needed to get the alcohol out of me."

First thought: he was in denial. One does not simply become an alcoholic because they love the taste of beer, there was an imbalance of some sort, something that pushed him to lead him this way. Mental illness had to have been the root of it all, why else would all these addicted patients be in the facility? They have become addicted to something, and it's psychological. That was not my place to say, or bring up, I barely knew the guy and I felt seriously heartbroken for him, but he needed to figure out his mind on his own terms, not from me.

"At least you're somewhere getting treatment though, it's better than being out in the world, continuing the same behavior, right?" I was attempting to make light out of a situation he clearly did not want to see through. I didn't want to apologize, I felt like when I apologized too much to someone it seemed phony, like it was a copout, so I didn't have to put thought into an actual response.

"Yeah, it's better than being off the rails but not what I expected, honestly though I've been in rehabs before and I never talk to people in em'. I keep to myself I'm kinda shy, people like to be nosey and I don't like it, but you got me to open up, it's actually nice talkin' to ya."

"Well I'm glad to hear I could help a little, I don't know… I guess it aids the process here to have a friend along the way." And I truly believed that, I was excited that we met, I was happy that I had someone to depend on while I was there, to sit with at meals. Seemed childish, but it was scary entering a whole new world, you never knew what to expect.

"Well that's a bit of my fucked life." I felt like that was my cue to explain my rendition of *a fucked-up life,* I just didn't know how or where to begin.

"So that means it's my turn, right? Well, unlike most people here I am not here because I struggle with an addiction, I'm clean. But my mind isn't the most stable…"

Chapter 11

Scarlet

"Honestly, I feel weird talking about myself, I don't like the idea of comparing my life to others, and having the ones I'm telling, compare my life to theirs, and others around them... if that makes any sense at all."

"I think I understand what you mean" Bryce said, with a not-so reassuring face.

"I just mean I don't want to spill my life all out on the table and then made to feel bad about it." It's hard to explain to someone how I've have felt and explain to him that I *didn't* want sympathy from what I told them, it was just a part of me.

"I ain't sitting in front of you to mock you." We held a stare at each other for a second and I cracked a smile.

"Alight, well I've been of the many people who are classified as depressed and with anxiety." I tried to speak normally of the subject, so it didn't seem like I was trying to receive some time of sympathetic response from the audience I was talking to. "It's gotten bad a few times, sophomore year pills were involved, but obviously I'm still here..." I took a pause because I could tell he didn't know where I was going to go from there. "From that point it only got worse, until I used another method junior year. With a ceiling fan and a scarlet colored scarf, the result was a lightheaded aftermath from a blackout, and a partially bruised neck." I took a deep breath, I realized what I had let out. That what I had just said what something I hadn't even told the counselors at Overbrooke, at least not in detail, I suddenly felt sick.

"I'm so sorry." I felt utterly disgusted that I disclosed that much information with him, for some reason It felt easy talking to him, the words flowed out of my mouth, it was as if he was the paper in one of my journals and the pen was just bursting with ink, all of my thoughts out on display. But, something like that isn't to be shared with the public and I regretted it instantly.

"Don't be… seems like ya needed to let that out"

"I just –

"Keep going" He cut me off, needing no more explanation.

"That's when I finally brought myself to realize that I needed help, from someone beyond me. I confronted my mom and we sorted things out…" He seemed so intrigued by my story.

"Fast forward a year later, for some reason things started to enter my mind violently again, I abruptly stopped taking my medicine and refused to take it. I didn't think I needed help anymore because I didn't think it mattered."

And I explained to him how *I couldn't do it*. How I took a shower to clear my mind and all it did was blend my tears in with a stream of water and muffle the sound of impeding thoughts. How when I got out *I still couldn't do it* and I paced and paced till I broke down, and how I faced my mom with a broken form of myself. How I was brought to a Hospital in the night…and I was kept in a very plain white room.

"And so, I ended up here, after evaluations, after interviews, and tests, the Hospital decided I couldn't be sent home." He was looking at me with his huge brown eyes, it was difficult for me to look at him throughout the telling of my story because it felt embarrassing, and degrading. "They knew I was a danger to myself and possibly people around me without some type of treatment."

He didn't have much to say initially, he was quiet for a little while after I finished, we both were.

"Yanno, if you need someone to talk to, I'm here. I knew some people who had thoughts like you, who had brains that didn't have correctly connected wires." He took a pause, seeming as if he might have had said something wrong. "I just mean I've had some close friends ruin their lives, take them away, and it's…uh pretty rough for all people involved." He took a sip of his coffee, but I stayed silent, I didn't think he was done speaking; anyway, I had been talking for a while and I didn't have much else to say. "Ya need to talk if those things get in your brain, look I can slip you my number, call me if you ever get a bad feeling, pick up the phone, I'll listen."

I just met him, yet he seemed to care if something negative overcame me. Not many people understood me, and for some odd reason it felt like *he did*. Bryce didn't judge me or degrade me for my reason behind being placed there, he supported me, encouraged me to reach out to him. We respected each other, and that's why we got along so well in the beginning.

"Thank you, really…" I gave him a simple smile, one that showed him I was grateful he was there to comfort me, but nothing that expressed I was overjoyed with the topic at hand. "You're the first person I have told about how I was placed here, well besides the people who work here of course, I don't plan on sharing my experience with anyone else in the facility."

He gave me a wilted smile, one that showed he cared and that he wanted to understand. One that showed *sympathy*, the one thing I never wanted from someone, but maybe from the right person it was needed.

Chapter 12

See ya Later

June 11th, was the next day spent in Overbrooke, it was the day I had a meeting set up with my parents. The women who had been my Social Worker there spoke to me about sitting both my parents down while I was there, and having a *so-called* intervention about my father, his drinking habits, and how it affected the family.

That wasn't something I haven't tried before... a few months previous to being admitted to the facility I dragged my father along to a therapy session with me. A week prior to bringing him, my therapist instructed me to write him a letter, explain everything I needed to in it, and lay everything out on paper, that way it would be easier to get my point across. So, when the time came I wrote a 12-page letter in my journal, and read it aloud to him, he acted like things would change around the house, but they didn't.

The differences with the facility intervention were that my Mom was present, and there were no more letters to be read, I said what I needed to say, frankly I didn't know what more I could do at that point.

At breakfast, Bryce and I sat together, I basically sat there watching him eat because that morning we were served scrambled eggs and I *really* do not enjoy them, I stuck to the fruit cup and my sugar cup filled with coffee.

"I might be leavin' today" Bryce told me with some egg still in his mouth.

"Ew, chew and swallow your food man" I laughed messing with him, my sarcastic nature comes natural with those I feel comfortable with, and he was someone I was okay around.

"Oh, like ya really care" he said with a glare in his eyes and a smirk across his chapped lips, the air was dry in here, my lips were chapped too. "I'm not sure what time, but uh yeah, the counselor told me I could probably go today."

It was rare for someone to stay less than 3 days, I guess it was because he expressed he'd like to be admitted to a rehab, rather than a Mental facility. I honestly think the facility just didn't want a bad *rep* though, he spoke pretty openly about how his admittance was wrong and misinterpreted. I guess releasing him earlier than most would save *them* the trouble.

I was told I would most likely able to be released that same day as well, after the meeting if all went well, and if I was feeling okay enough. Since my parents would be there, and a plan would be set up as a family, I would probably be released.

"Wow, it's crazy that they're letting you leave so early, but I may be released today too, after the meeting; I don't want to get my hopes up though, I'm not trying to jinx anything."

I was afraid he was going to be released while I was in the meeting, that he would leave without a goodbye, he was important to me now, for some reason I felt like this wasn't over, that it couldn't be over.

"Hopefully, so when we both get out we can see each other" he folded up a small piece of paper and slid it to me cautiously, I opened it and it was a slip of paper with his number on it, so I had some way to contact him.

"Reese Emery?" My social worker was standing in the doorway waiting for me. "Are you ready? Your parents are here." I wasn't ready, it was so sudden, I reacted abruptly.

"No, can I have a minute, I just want to finish my fruit and then go to the bathroom really quick." I panicked, I needed to give myself a little more time.

"Sure, try to be fast." She turned around and headed down the hall toward her office, where I assume my parents were waiting for me.

The picture I had begun coloring the first day and finished yesterday was sitting in the middle of the table, so I reached for it. I took a red marker, since it was the closest writing utensil to me and flipped the coloring page over, I wrote down my full name and my number as well, so he had a way to contact me. I handed him the page, color side up and said, "My gift to you."

He accepted it and said, "It's beautiful, thank you." I laughed because it was just a coloring I had done but it was sweet, and I was glad he cared, or at least *pretended* to. We just looked at each other and he hugged me. We weren't supposed to, I assume, but no one was around to see, the Dayroom was dry.

"I asked for extra time because I needed to give you that, just in case you were gone when I came back. I finished my fruit a while ago, and my bladder can wait." I smiled

Without any word he scanned the room, looking to see who was around us, no patients were in the Dayroom, and even though the room had windows spanning across the front, facing the main desk which the workers occupy, they were all focused on their tasks. I guess files and things, I don't know what thy could be so intently working on, but they weren't focused on us that was for sure.

He kissed me.

It was sudden and quick, but I sort of felt it coming when he glanced around the room, looking for other humans that could witness what was about to occur.

I didn't come to Overbrooke looking to find someone to kiss, I came here because I lost a part of myself. But meeting him felt like what I needed, we could help each other; we could support each other.

I smiled wide and I could feel myself blushing. I stepped back and looked around us frantically, trying to see if someone was waiting to reprimand us for what had just happened, but it was just us.

"That paper, don't lose it" I told him pointing to the geometric sun and the moon.

"I won't" he glanced down as he spoke. "I had to do that, I didn't know if that would have to be it for now, I didn't know if I would leave when you went in."

I gave him a smirk and started to walk away, toward the exit of the Dayroom, "Bye Bryce."

"No, see ya later." I shook my head and smiled with relief as I walked out.

Chapter 13

Painting Trees

My release day is a date I will never forget, simply because it marked a day that I overcame something when my mind was ridden with doubt; an aspect of myself I was unsure if I could overcome.

When I left the Social Worker's room after the bogus intervention, if you could really call it an intervention, Bryce had already left, but he made sure to leave a note on the Dayroom table for me;

"Reese, I'll see you later."

I slipped it into my sweatshirt pocket before leaving the room to go pack my things from room 23 to go home, to my real home.

Walking outside of Overbrooke and into my Mom's vehicle was one of the most satisfying feeling in a while. The breeze hitting my hair, and the heat from the sun touching my pale skin, it felt surreal, and I wasn't even in the facility comparably long to some of the patients there. I couldn't imagine how they were surviving it.

My parents brought me to Five Guys Burgers and Fries as my "complimentary congratulations for getting released from a Mental Hospital". They knew it was a place I absolutely loved. I never made it a habit of going there previously because of the fattening stigma it has, it was a once in blue moon thing, and it happened to be a special blue moon night. I made sure to fill up on my loaded bacon cheese burger and stuff my face with fries. Not the most nutritious meal to enter my body, but definitely one well deserved. The comparison of the Hospital food and Psychiatric food to what I was eating then, was unbelievably drastic. Being in the facility I didn't complain much about what I was given, I ate what looked okay and left alone what I knew I wouldn't be satisfied with. But before being admitted I hadn't been eating much. My mind was focused on other things. I lose appetite in times of distress. When I was being fed in the facility, I was so hungry that I didn't think too much about the difference between what I was previously used to and what I was eating then. I don't think I left a scrap on the tray, every inch of the burger was gone and I made sure to stock up on as many fries as I could, making sure to take sip breaks of my Dr. Pepper in between, because I'm known to drown my food in salt, especially French fries. After devouring my meal, we gathered back in the car to head home. My parents couldn't stop telling me how happy they were that I was back, and I was happy too.

In the car, I was focused on the pattern of speed the car was going, measuring it against the trees, watching how they blended together making it look like a mosaic painting, it was beautiful, something I would never take for granted again.

Chapter 14

Trinkets and Memories

In all honesty, I was racing the clock to get home, so I could get in touch with Bryce, I was hoping to talk to him outside of the facility. I was free now, and so was he, the idea of staying in contact with someone I met inside of a Mental facility struck me as something that probably wasn't the best idea, because we both had things we needed to focus on of course, but I didn't struggle with addiction, and he and I seemed to be the type to help mend each other along the way.

When I arrived at my house, I took it all in; I stepped out of the car slowly, staring at the yellow panels on the house. The red shutters, framing the window my dog was peeking through waiting for all of us to step inside, I missed him like crazy. He was a fuzzy white ball of energy, and I named him Bear because when he was a puppy he was so tiny, but his paws seemed too big for his body, like Bear paws.

Grabbing my journal, since I had carried it out of the facility with me, I shut the car door and walked past the abandoned yellow Volkswagen Beetle that I had left behind, it made me smile, I hated that car but seeing it meant I was home. Entering the garage and into my kitchen, I took in the scent around me and loved every second of it. My dog came running into me full speed, begging for me to pick him up and greet him. I missed the comfort of my own home, it was an indescribable feeling being able to come back to the place that was the foundation of my existence.

I walked through my house slowly, deepening my connection with the objects around me, the last time I was in this space, I was in such a fogged mind space, I didn't want anything to continue, and in that moment, I was grateful they had. I headed to my room and dropped on my bed, soaking in the covers, burying myself in warmth. My own bed was something I missed most, it was something I never wanted to give up again. I laid there for a while, just thinking about how happy I was to be back. Laying there I was content, but it felt like I was missing something. Then I realized how long it had been since I used my phone, my bed was a prominent place for me to utilize my phone, so I remembered what I had been missing, and realized how dead it probably was; I reluctantly sat up from my bed, but grabbed a throw blanket and wrapped it around my shoulders, the imagery on the throw was Spiderman, it was a gift from Malory a few birthdays' ago. I got up with my cape dragging along the floor and carried myself to the kitchen, where I presumed my parents had left my phone to stay while I was gone. Low and behold, I was correct, it was sitting on the countertop next to the microwave; I picked it up and headed back to my room, attempting to turn it on even though I could have bet money on what the result from holding down that power button would be. It didn't turn on, so when I got to my room, I plugged it into the outlet below my window, the one that faced the front of my house, it's the only outlet that when I plugged my phone into, it would still reach my bed. I need to let it charge up before I could fully turn it on and use it for Bryce related reasons. Waiting for it to charge up was a process I knew I didn't want to sit through but had to, I laid back down in my bed and started to examine my bedroom, look at all the pictures on the wall and remember the memories associated with them all. Finding all my treasures and trinkets I kept for decoration and memories, I was so absorbed in the contents of my room that when I dozed off they transpired into my dreams. I guess I was way too comfortable in my own bed to not fall asleep.

Chapter 15

(Maybe: Bryce)

With no one to disturb me I slept for about two hours, my mom had to go straight to work once we got home, and my Father, well I have no idea where he was, but it never concerned me, I didn't focus on his actions anymore, they were at his expense, not mine, so what did I care? When I woke up I was tangled in a sea of blankets and huddled up next to Bear by my side, whenever other people were home he paid no attention to me, but when he realized everyone was gone except me, he always rushed to my side. I had this theory that he only wanted to show me affection when no one was around because I'm his mom, Yanno how teenagers are embarrassed to be around their parents, but in a dog sort of way, I more or less told myself that, so I didn't feel hated by him.

I unraveled myself from the mess I was in and attempted not to disturb my dog, but it was inevitable, I woke him up, and when I did, he was quite unhappy. I reached over him to grab my phone, I pulled the cord out of the charging port and watched my phone light up, I looked at the percentage and saw it has risen to 100%. Meaning I had to have been asleep for multiple hours. I looked at the time and it read 6:08 pm of course. I honestly had no idea when I arrived home because I wasn't focused on times I was worried about life around me. I had an abundance of missed messages, old social media notifications and I ignored most of them, the social media ones at least. I had multiple texts from Malory, my sister Haley and my other friend Addison; I took a look at all of them and didn't respond to any. Malory was just updating me on life for when I was released, telling me about school happenings and telling me she couldn't wait till I was back home. Addison left a ton of messages, worried out of her mind, demanding I answer and talk to her, Malory had told everyone I was super sick in the Hospital and my mom wouldn't allow me to have my phone, so this must have been prior to her knowing of that *false* but *affective* story. And my sister's messages consisted of her telling me she loved me and that she wanted me to get in touch with her as soon as I was released.

When Haley found out where I was and what happened she was ecstatic, and not in the happy way. She was furious no one had told her about everything the day it actually happened, she found out the next day, at night time I believe. Haley swore she would've been there, that she would've come from Massachusetts to see me and stay with me until I was *better*. It was thoughtful, and very much like her character (toward me at least, she was extremely protective). But even if she did know about everything the initial day it happened, her coming here wouldn't have made a difference. I was still unstable, no one in my family could've done anything to ease what was happening in my head, I think she felt like she could've help mend the pain, but no one could.

I made a reminder on my phone to call Haley, I didn't have the energy to sit there and talk for an elongated amount of time about what happened and how I was feeling, I wasn't in the mood to have a sister to sister therapy session. I just got done talking about my feelings endlessly for multiple days in a row, I was striving for a release from that, I needed a break.

I pulled down the notification bar on my phone and saw two last messages were sent to me. It was a number I hadn't had in my phone yet; the iPhone can detect who the sender might be by the name stated in the message sent. The message on top had a phone number above it, the notification under it was labeled *(Maybe: Bryce)*.

I assumed he told me it was him the first message, hence the labeled name on top, so I opened both and read what he sent.

"Hey, it's Bryce, not sure when you're getting out but hopefully soon." I noticed he used the wrong *you're*, which made me laugh a little. The second message went like this:

"I'm glad we met, I hope I can see you later today." I hoped the same, my parents weren't home any longer to stay with me, so I figured why not make plans to see him? I had just gotten out, but so had he, we could celebrate together, and get to know each other outside of Overbrooke.

I was nervous to reach back out to him, I knew he was the one to initially contact me but now this was real life, I wasn't closed in a box anymore, neither of us were. We became free, and so did our minds. After a few moments of dwelling on the idea of contacting him back or not, I realized we had a good connection, and even if we didn't end up seeing each other that day, we would still be able to catch up.

I typed out a message to him:

"Hey Bryce, sorry I didn't get to you sooner, I spent some time with my family, and took some time to get reacquainted with my bed haha, my phone also needed some battery, but I'm here now." I stared at the message and read it over and over and over again until the words didn't seem like words anymore and it looked like a messy scrabble board. I was sick of rereading it and trying to figure out if it sounded dumb, so I just sent it. Honestly, I knew nothing bad would happen, it was just a message, I was being way too dramatic about the situation.

Bryce answered almost instantaneously, about a minute went by and he replied:

"I didn't know if you were ignoring me, happy to know you're not" again using the wrong *you're* but I didn't have the heart to tell him, I also didn't want to look like the asshole grammar police that literally everyone despises, so I let it be. As I was getting ready to type out another message to him, my phone started ringing. The name popped up (*Maybe: Bryce*) because I hadn't added him to my contacts yet, I was caught up in the texts and didn't even think of it. I answered, and it was crazy to hear his voice over the phone. "What's up Darlin". That's something he always called me, and I absolutely loved it, I think he did it as a joke at first, when I teased him about country music, but it became a term of endearment, and I smiled every time I heard him say it.

I laughed and said, "just sitting home alone, my parents left so I'm doing nothing".

"Hmm sounds exciting, why don't you come to see me? I'll be at the Walmart in your town, you can meet me there, then we can drive back to where I'm staying."

"That sounds good to me, just text me and update me when you get there, and I'll meet you."

"Sure thing, I'll see ya later."

"See you later Bryce."

Then I hung up the phone and glanced over our messages before completely removing myself from bed. When I sat up I looked directly into the mirror that was sat in front of me, my vanity was next to my bed, so when I propped myself up I could see myself. I threw my hair up into a pony tail and smiled wide into my reflection, thinking that Bryce and I were actually going to meet up, spend some real time together, not organized time.

I bent down and started to slip on my checkered vans, when I looked back up into my reflection a tear escaped. Because I was real, and I was alive, and I made that happen. I was starting to get back on track, and I thought Bryce would be too, it was a good place.

Chapter 16

Walmart Tracks

Getting back into a car and driving felt incredible. I had the ability to go where ever I wanted, a car full of gas, the roads were open, and a will to move on from the past. It was empowering to be behind the wheel again, such a simple task, but an important one.

I laid pressure onto the break and moved the gear into reverse, and pulled out of the driveway, making my way to the main road. Waiting for cars passing I turned on music, something I hadn't been able to do in a little while.

Iris, by the Goo Goo Dolls came on, and I let it play on, my favorite song definitely had time in my day. When there was free space to make my way onto the open road, I did so. Turned my car left and headed straight for Walmart, where Bryce would be waiting for me.

~

When I got there, I looped around the parking lot looking for him, I saw him sitting in the bed of a black Chevy pickup truck, I pulled into the spot directly next to him. He immediately hopped off the truck and rushed to my door, I unlocked it and he pulled it open. He took off his sunglasses and I looked into his eyes, smiling. He leaned in and met his lips against mine. When he pulled away he smirked at me, "What's up Beautiful?" Ive never felt comfort like that before, I've never had someone want to be in my presence like that before. And him calling me beautiful didn't seem like a random adjective to make me fall for him, it seemed genuine, he seemed real. It felt real.

"I'm doing pretty great, how are you?" I said with a giggle in my voice, I was stoked to be there with him.

"Better now, I'm just waiting for JT he's still inside, I'm not sure what he's up to, impossible to keep tabs on that kid anymore." JT was his brother, older brother. That's who he was staying with, JT had been on a bad track with drugs in the past. Heroin was his poison, but he was 'clean' apparently, and supported Bryce's recovery, as he should have.

Some time passed, and Bryce and I just talked, caught up within the few hours we had been home from Overbrooke. While in the facility we joked about how we would light up a blunt together when we got out. Bryce brought it up in our catching up session. "So, about that blunt?" I laughed, I was by no means a stoner, not a regular smoker, and had never attempted other drugs. The occasional bud was okay with me though, a smooth buzz was nice. I wasn't exactly sure if he was serious though.

"Are you kidding or?" I had a perplexed face for sure, nothing that screamed uninterested but not anything that seemed overeager.

"I'm serious, when we get back to my house we can get some, only if you want to." Weed to me, has always been no big deal; non-addictive, it's never taken lives, and compared to everything else out there, it was harmless.

"Alright I'm down."

As we were finishing up our conversation Bryce spotted his older brother in the distance, "Finally, JT has been found". While we were in Overbrooke I had a brief look at JT, he came to visit Bryce the same night my mom came to see me. We sat at the same table during visiting time, super far apart, but still the same vicinity. So, I had seen his brother before. He was tall, scrawny, long beard with gray streaks throughout. He looked a little rough when I first saw him visiting Bryce but standing significantly further away from him in the Walmart parking lot, he seemed way worse than before.

I couldn't exactly put my finger on how he looked, or on how he was walking. He slumped his shoulders like he hadn't slept in weeks, his eyes drooped to match his posture, he looked absolutely miserable. Definitely different from my first impression of him. I glanced over to Bryce who was standing to the left of me, leaning against my car and he looked horrified. I didn't say a word, I felt like I was about to witness something I shouldn't.

"Motherfucker" Bryce said it under his breath, rather aggressively, and I knew it was directed toward his brother. I was still lost on the idea of what was happening before me, but I knew it wasn't right.

I felt like I should speak up, ask if everything was okay but I was tongue tied. Bryce spoke up to me, instead of me confronting him, I felt like an idiot for just standing there silent, but he probably knew I had no idea what to say.

"I'm going to fuck him up" before I could respond to his statement he spoke again "Get back in your car, close the windows, and I apologize for my faggot brother". Stunned I started walking to the driver's side of my car, I turned quick before he could leave my side and I responded "Is everything okay?" and of course that's the statement I use, because obviously everything is *NOT* okay, but I didn't know how else to phrase it, and I was worried, panicked.

"No, he's high off his ass right now, he's supposed to be sober, and I'm staying with him, and this is what he does, at a Walmart?!" With a lump in my throat, I backed into my car and Bryce shut the door, motioning for me to roll up the windows. I did as he told. And I sat there, thinking, watching.

Bryce took JT by the front of his white T-shirt, grabbed him at the chest and threw him to the bed of the pickup truck, I remember the bang of his head on the Chevy vividly. JT rolled onto his side, or at least was attempting to, he could barely move his limbs. He laid there, almost completely still. Bryce was standing over him with pain in his eyes, I could tell how much anger he was harboring inside. It felt like a few minutes passed while JT just laid there still, before Bryce did or said anything, like he was building everything up inside, getting ready to explode.

His face started to well up, his neck bulging with veins and his eyes glistened over, he started to scream. My windows were up, and I had music on, but I could hear him clear as day.

"GET YOUR FUCKING ASS UP YOU PIECE OF SHIT" I jolted as soon as his voice left his mouth, I wasn't expecting the volume to resonate as it did. It echoed, and I looked down trying to pretend I didn't hear it. There was a pause, so I looked over my shoulder to see what was happening, Bryce was still standing over him, same position, same terrifying face. JT still had not moved, laying there, looking lifeless, my heart was racing I was sitting in my car with no way to assist anyone, I didn't know if he needed help, I was clueless, in complete shock.

Bryce grabbed onto JT's calves and started to pull him from the bed of the truck, finally JT had the slightest bit of life brought back into him, his started to lift up his torso, trying to move himself off the truck, instead of being dragged by Bryce. His eyes were constantly going in and out. Open, close, open, close, every other second it was different. He propped himself up, sitting against the side of the bed of the truck.

"You think you can fuck everyone else's life up around you, we didn't come here so you could make a track on your arm, we have a young girl here, she's my girlfriend, and YOU HAVE KIDS. Get the fuck in the car." There was no way in hell JT was getting himself up on his own. Bryce had to wrap him around his body, basically dragging him to the passenger side of the truck. I was honestly surprised Bryce didn't drop him on the concrete, he seemed so infuriated.

All the while this was happening I just had a pit in my stomach, a lump in my throat. I felt absolutely horrific. I felt terrible that Bryce had just been released from Overbrooke and had the idea he was going to be staying in a clean, safe environment, but apparently that was not the case. Bryce had to take control of the driver's seat, and I would have to follow him back to JT's home. Before Bryce got settled into the seat he made his way over to my yellow bug.

I was used to yelling, weird behavior and anger in my household. My father was the cause of most of it, and even though I grew up with the noise, and the violence, I never became immune to it. I'm not sure if other people do but I sure never did. Every time someone yells I cringe a little harder, every time I hear a bang I shield myself a bit tighter, it just becomes more terrifying. I hate the noise anger carries. I hated seeing Bryce harbor that hate, and I understood why he acted the way he did, I just wish it didn't have to be done.

He motioned for me to open the door, I did so. He could realize my tension. "Are you okay? I am sorry you hada see that, he's supposed to be clean couldn't believe he ain't." I smiled at him, understanding he meant no harm, and nothing was directed toward me, but it was nice he apologized anyway. He told me to follow closely behind him on the parkway, that it wouldn't be too long, only about a thirty-minute drive. I nodded in agreement, so he knew I was on board with his plan and his kissed my forehead to let me know he was there to comfort me.

Chapter 17

Car Hopping

If I had to rate the driving experience from a zero to a ten, I'd have to give it a hard six. I had to knock off significant points for Bryce's brother jumping out of the car right before we got onto the parkway to hit up the liquor store. And making us wait on the side of the road for him. Not a pleasant experience, not one I would recommend, and not one I'd volunteer to be a part of again. Let me set this scenario up for you a little clearer.

Leaving Walmart, it was a smooth exit, the parkway entrance is not too far away, I'd say roughly about four minutes. As we approached the stop light right before the parkway entrance I see JT becoming restless in the pickup in front of me, squinting to try and get a clearer image of what was going on, I could see JT was taking off his seatbelt and attempting to unlock his passenger side door. Bryce was screaming at him, still trying to pay close attention to the road ahead in case the light turned green.

In one swift motion, JT unlatched the door hopped out and started to run across the street to a plaza nearby. He didn't even look both directions before crossing the street it was a miracle he wasn't squashed by a car in the process, it's a decently busy road he was running across. The door was still wide open, Bryce stretched his arm over as the light turned green and pulled the door closed, before he pushed the gas, right on the entrance to the parkway he pulled over, I followed his lead, completely boggled at what just happened.

While pulled over Bryce switched on his hazards and I did the same, as I assumed that was the correct thing to do in that type of situation. He removed himself from the truck and entered my wimpy car, furious, I swear I could've seen the steam brewing off of him, it was pretty insane. When he sat next to me he didn't even say anything to, he was franticly attempting to call his brother, over and over again. When he called him, what felt like about eight times and he never picked up, he finally put down the phone and turned toward me. I looked at him with a worried approach on my face. He just seemed like he wanted to put his fist through a wall, or JT's face.

"I'm so incredibly sorry about this, this was not how it was supposed to go for me." He honestly seemed apologetic, and I knew it wasn't his fault. By no means was I mad about the situation, a little worried, sure, but mad was not the emotion.

"You don't have to be sorry for an action you can't control." I took his hand in mine to show him I was there, that I wasn't going anywhere and that I cared.

"He was running to the liquor store" he seemed guilty, as if he was the one who told him to do it.

"That's what I was wondering, there's a dance studio, a liquor store, and a pizzeria in that plaza, so I had a hunch for where he was headed. Why is he going there?" I didn't want to blatantly ask if it was for him, and I didn't want to think it was. And by the look he had on his face that I could see through his rearview mirror in the pickup while JT was trying to escape, it didn't seem like Bryce was a part of the plan.

"I don't really know Darlin', I don't want you to freak out or get angry but I'm pretty sure he's getting liquor for me, so I don't go through any withdrawal symptoms." I instantly sank into my seat, I didn't want to be sucked into that, I didn't want to meet that end of him, and he told me I never should.

"I don't want to drink it though, I have no intentions of sipping it, he's just flipping out at the moment, he's so high he doesn't know what's up from down."

Relief settled into my bones. Knowing there was going to be liquor in the house bothered me, but maybe if Samantha put it out of sight he wouldn't even think to take a swig of it. (Samantha is JT's fiancé.)

I peep out the side mirror and see JT stumbling up the parkway entrance with a black plastic bag. Bryce wasn't paying attention, I tapped on his shoulder and motioned behind us to the right and there he was. Bryce jumped out of the car and raced over to his brother, telling him he was an idiot, and asking him what he was thinking hopping out of the truck at a red light, into the middle of the road. JT was shoved back into the Chevy and then we were finally on our way to the house.

The rest of the drive was perfectly fine, it was pleasant, easy, not too long. I just turned up my music and cruised along behind Bryce. If the car hopping incident didn't occur the drive would've been a ten, but like I said, shaved off points for a terrible encounter.

Chapter 18

Hayden and Josie

Getting to where Bryce was staying was a relief, when we pulled up to a storage unit I was a tad confused. We parked by what looked like the office of the unit, and I got out of my car, walked over to him. Two kids came running outside of the door, I knew JT and Samantha had daughters, but I never really thought much of it. Kids and I usually don't get along, so I tried to block that aspect of his stay out of my mind. I realized there must be an apartment type of situation attached to the office of the storage unit and that's where they had been living.

The two young girls automatically lit up when they saw their Uncle. Bryce had told me about them, how he loved his nieces, and I could tell the bond they shared when we showed up. The older daughter ran to Bryce's arms, begging for him to pick her up. I watched all this from afar, with a smile on my face. It was amazing to see that these two little girls have so much love for their Uncle, so much love for someone I was falling for. Bryce looked over his shoulder at me and waved me over, suggesting coming toward them, since I was still standing by the opposite side of the car. I approached, and he introduced me to the young girls. "Reese, this is Josie, and the little one is Hayden." I smiled at them, thinking they would honestly ignore my presence like most children do, but the youngest ran over and gave me a hug. I bent down and reciprocated, Josie followed in her lead, pulling her younger sister off of my legs to get her own time to embrace me.

"Well it's nice to meet you two." I said with a little laugh in the tone of my voice. Still in shock these children were so outgoing, so ready to welcome me. Josie started jumping up and down, seeming very excited, like she had something to tell me.

"Ooo can you come inside and play with us?" I didn't have a second to respond before their mother stepped in.
"Josie get the fuck out of her way, leave her alone." But honestly, I wasn't being bothered, I kind of enjoyed that a kid was enjoying my presence. It made my stay seem more welcomed.

"Oh, it's okay, I don't mind" I told Samantha, keeping eye contact with Josie though, feeling slightly wrong to say it directly to Samantha. "Maybe a little later we can play." Her face lit up again and she looked at Hayden, telling her that we could play tons of games in a little bit, both of them were excited. Samantha shooed them back inside and told Josie to look after Anna, their littlest sister I assumed. Josie ran inside in almost a panicked state, as if she forgot her sister was still in the house, unaccompanied. Hayden followed in her steps, running up the stairs right behind her.

Bryce was smiling as they entered the house, I could tell they all had a strong bond. "I fucking love those kids." It made me feel all warm inside when he said that. I think him expressing his emotions made me happy, it showed that he didn't have to use a substance to alter his emotion, that he was a real person, with real feelings and thoughts. And those kids obviously loved the heck out of him.

Chapter 19

Get your shit together

And so, our night began, I was hoping I would spend time with Bryce, get to be with him and get to know how he was in the outside world, but that idea shifted as the night went on. We entered their home and I was again greeted by two young girls. Josie, the oldest begged me to play with them, Bryce whispered in my ear to go entertain them, it caught me off guard a little, but I would help anyway I could. I went into their very tiny room and spent time with Hayden and Josie. I knew I had to keep them focused on me, and talking, because of what was going on outside of their room.

JT had been acting strange and I knew it pertained to his heroin addiction. It baffled me that two young girls had to be around something so insane. I felt for them, and somehow connected with them. I knew what it was like to have a parent off the rocker, someone who put a substance before their own children.

Heroin addicts aren't bad people per-say, I don't think I believe anyone is truly bad, everyone does what they think is right for them. I bet JT didn't want to be controlled by a substance, any more than Bryce wanted to be controlled by a bottle. It just pained me to sit there with two young girls, who I later learned was seven and the youngest three.

I have never been good with kids, frankly many kids don't enjoy my company. It's a miracle if I'm handed a child and they don't instantly burst into tears right before my eyes. But these girls seemed to bond with me, we had a connection. Josie, I could tell had to grow up fast, looking after both her sisters at the ripe age of only seven. Her youngest sister was only a few months, not even a year yet, and she was held with the responsivity of feeding her, calming her down, entertaining her. It was like Samantha and JT didn't know how to function properly without Josie there as their sidekick.

As I was in the room with the girls, they told me about their night time routine, and movies they recently watched, one of them being the movie "Sing", it's about talking animals that create a singing show. Im honestly not much of an expert on the film, I have never seen it.

It was hard to pay attention and focus on the children I was sitting with, and supposed to be entertaining because I was focused on the dialogue coming from the kitchen. I was fixated on Bryce's voice scolding JT.

"Get your shit together man, I can't believe you're acting this way right now."
There was never a response from JT but you could tell by the tone in Samantha and Bryce's voice that him not responding pissed them off to no end.

I was snapped out of the kitchen dialogue when I realized a child had leaped into my lap. Hayden was sitting there, looking up at me, begging me to go into the living room with them to watch "Sing". I knew that I was supposed to keep them sheltered from what was going on but it was hard to just tell her no, I essentially have no authority over those kids, they don't even know me. I begged them to stay in the room while I "went to the bathroom" which was code for going to talk to Bryce.

I entered the kitchen cautiously and Samantha was talking to JT sternly "Motherfuker, open your eyes, I can't deal with this bullshit right now." And Bryce was busy tiding up the counters, I think he was prepping to make something to eat. I walked through the entrance and swiveled passed JT sitting on a chair nodding out, and was met by Bryce. I told him I didn't know what to do.

"So, the girls want out of the room and I don't know what to do, I can't really tell them no but I also know they should probably stay there." He looked a little confused. He took a look behind me then spoke.

"Are they in the room, did you leave them?" I shook my head in agreement realizing that probably was not my best decision.

He pushed passed me and entered the room to talk to the girls. Josie and Hayden lit up when they saw their Uncle Bryce; this automatically plastered a smile across my face. His interaction with them was remarkable. He attempted to reason with them and explain they needed to stay in the room for a little while longer because "Mommy and Daddy needed alone time".

Apparently, Samantha heard the conversation and had a few words of input for them. "I don't give a shit if they're out here, JT is being an asswipe, they can stay in the living room if they stop whining." Bryce picked up Hayden and I escorted Josie out, as we left the room Bryce had a word of advice.

"You hear that? Leave your mom alone." And for some reason the entire situation made my heart sink to my stomach, I felt sick. It seemed like Samantha had no intentions of interacting with her kids, to comfort them, but then again, I don't know anything, I don't know much about children and the way functional families work, I was never a part of one, I just assumed it was the opposite of how my household worked. But this wasn't the opposite side of the spectrum this was just a whole other ball park.

Bryce handed Josie the remote as they sat on the couch and he asked me to stay seated with them, I did as I was asked. And the movie began to play, and the two girls were silent, deeply in tune with what was happening on the screen. A few minutes passed and Bryce peeked around the corner, motioning for me to enter the kitchen. I hopped of the sofa and headed his way.

"I'm sorry you have to stay with them, but to get away can you take a ride with Sam to pick up the bud." I was a little defeated, I just wanted to be able to spend time with him.

I responded "Okay, where are you going." He motioned with his index finger toward the floor, meaning he was going to be staying at the house. "Why?" it was a dumb question I just didn't think before I spoke sometimes.

"JT can't be left alone with the kids, and he can't be in a car, god forbid Sam got pulled over, she already doesn't have a license."

I couldn't say no to him, I mean I could've, but it would've been a dick move, so I agreed to take a ride with Sam. Honestly, she intimidated me a little bit, she was definitely someone I would describe as being a hard-ass, but I was hoping she would be a little different around me since we had just met. She was just a very blunt human, she didn't beat around the bush, which I mean, could be a blessing and a curse.

Bryce pulled me in for a hug and kissed me atop the head. He patted my back to motion for me to follow Samantha, "Is she coming with me?" Sam blurted.

"Yeah, I am" I responded, so Bryce didn't have to.

"Alright then let's get the fuck outta here then." We walked down the stairs and out toward the Chevy, I sat down in the passenger seat and before I knew it we were on our way.

Chapter 20

Bud

I wasn't familiar with the town we were in. South Jersey hadn't had much of an impact on my life, so I had no direction in which we were going. All I know is that Sam kept saying the cops are vicious out there and that we couldn't get pulled over, or we'd be screwed, big time. She tried to imitate conversation with me, I guess so the car ride wouldn't be awkward, but honestly silence doesn't bother me.

"So, you and Bryce, interesting...". How does one respond to a comment like that? I shook my head in agreement and then spoke up. "Yeah, I don't know, we just kind of connected." We did, I didn't have any other explanation to our partnership.

"No, I think it's a great thing, Bryce is a hand full when he's drinking but he means well, he's a good guy." She paused when she made a turn down a dark street, then continued to talk. "He means well I think, I just hope he stays well this time, all I'm saying is to be careful, I don't want a young girl like you to ruin your heart." Again, I had no idea how to respond to that, but it didn't have to, because she began to speak again. "How old are you again?"

"I'm eighteen." I know I was young and I didn't have to be told it to know it, even though Bryce was eight years older than me it didn't seem like he was, my level of intellectuality didn't seem far off from his, sometimes I actually wondered if *he* understood *me*.

"Then you're still in school, right?" and she was correct, I was still a senior in high school.

"Yes, a senior, but I graduate soon."

We were both silent for a little bit, and the car had no music playing, I guess Samantha realized the lack of tunes when we both grew silent. She inched her hand over toward the radio and turned on some music, it was country.

"Do you like country music?" Sam asked me in question.

"Umm, honestly not my top pick of genre but I don't hate any music, I just choose to not listen to country very often."

"What a bummer country music is great, JT and I are actually going to a county concert next month, were bringing Bryce along with us, I know you don't love the music, but you should come with us, it'll be a good time." It was nice of her to offer me to spend time with them, made me feel like she enjoyed my presence.

"I would be totally down to go, I absolutely love concerts, doesn't matter what kind, I'm sure I'll learn to fall in love with the music I have a month's time." It wasn't a lie, I do love concerts and most music I could handle, even though country wasn't my first choice of music, I'm sure I'd still have a blast.

"Great, I'm not sure the exact details all I know is that it's next month, but I'll be sure to have Bryce fill you in."

"Sounds good to me!" I smiled in agreement, letting her know I was actually interested, even though she was driving she glanced over to see my reaction.

~

We kept driving, we were on the road for what felt like 15 minutes, not too long. We were turning down a remote road where she said the dealer would be. In all honesty, I've only been on one *drug run,* but it was with kids my age, which was not as intimidating as someone older. We were also not in the best area for staying discreet from the police, I was a little nervous, but I trusted that Samantha had successfully bought drugs before, I knew this hadn't been her first rodeo. We pulled up to a street corner next to a stop sign and a Hispanic man hopped in the back seat. He had a heavy build, short buzzed hair, and he looked like a normal guy in his twenties. I would have never suspected that he dealt drugs, the kids that had been in my school look like drug dealers, this guy *looked* innocent, but I guess some of the most innocent individuals have the deepest secrets. They had a quick chat as Samantha looped around the block and handed him money in exchange for the weed. I never caught his name, he probably went by something other than his real name on the streets, to keep his identity safe'; at least that would be the smart thing to do. We ended where we started and dropped him back off, and we were on our way back.

The ride back to her house was pretty quiet, we didn't say much, which in all honesty I kind of enjoyed I wasn't in the mood to talk about my life with her, I wasn't too interested. It took another 15 minutes to arrive back at the storage unit/apartment and when we arrived Bryce was sitting outside with JT on the curb.

Chapter 21

Look at the stars

Bryce looked distraught when we arrived, and JT didn't look much healthier than when we left. When we stepped out of the car Samantha approached JT with a stern voice, "If you don't snap the fuck out of it you're not smoking with us."

Bryce shook his head in agreement and flicked his cigarette into the street.

"Let's go in the house, we can roll it in the kitchen and come back out to smoke." Bryce said, and so I followed his lead. We opened up the door and entered the apartment, the girls were already in bed so that difficulty was already sorted out.

We walked over to table in the kitchen and Samantha took out the weed, and then laid it on the table. Bryce dragged JT up the stairs and made him sit at the far end of the table. Bryce took out a Dutch to roll the weed in, he chopped the guts out of the Dutch and pushed them onto a paper towel on the table, to carefully dispose of them in the garbage. He set the gutted Dutch on the side of the table and began to break up the weed. It was sticking to his fingers while he was crushing it, but I guess it didn't faze him. He made a taco shape out of the white computer paper he broke it up on and poured the remains of the crushed weed in the Dutch wrapper. He licked the wrapper and rolled it together. The masterpiece was finished.

Samantha handed him a lighter and we were ready to smoke. We left JT in the kitchen, he was passed out on the table, it was best that way.

We headed outside, and Bryce took a seat on the curb, Samantha stood behind him and stretched her arm over his shoulder for him to hand her the blunt. He lit the blunt then passed it back. She took two puffs and handed it back to Bryce. He took a big hit and handed it to me. I held the blunt in my hand and looked at it. It was rolled pretty well, I mean I don't know the technique of rolling a blunt per say but it looked pretty good to me.

I held the blunt to my lips, wrapped them around the end and took a hit, I pulled the drag into my chest feeling it go down my throat into my lungs, I didn't hold it for long, I felt a cough coming on, so I blew out, releasing the smoke into the air. Then I coughed, trying to hold it back so I didn't look like a wimp. Then I handed it back to Bryce and sat down on the curb next to him in the process.

Then we kept passing it around. Samantha took two more hits then called it quits, she said she had to go inside and make sure JT wasn't fucking anything up. So, for the first time all day, it was just us. Bryce and me. At this point I'd taken about 5 hits, and I didn't know in the moment I was feeling it, but oh lord was I feeling it.

Everything and nothing started to make sense all at the same time.

I thought about the night we were having and the jokes we had talked about throughout the day, and everything felt amazing, I felt free, like nothing could stop me, like nothing could stop us.

We ended up walking down the driveway and around the parking lot, I was too jittery to stay still and sit around I needed to let out my energy. I was standing on the outside of him, closer to the street, he looked at me and said, "Can you do me a favor?" I nodded in agreement. "Can you switch sides with me?"

I told him I would, and we switched places, "Why did you do that?" I asked.

He turned to me again and told me to keep me safe. I still didn't understand what he meant, I was lost... and high as a kite. "You've never heard of that? The girl stands on the inside toward the curb."

"No, why is that?" I questioned him.

"Because if a car were passing, you'd be safe, the man is supposed to stand on the outside as a protector for the women." I lit up, that was the sweetest thing I'd ever heard.

I looked toward him and planted a kiss on him, letting him know I appreciated it, and him. We walked back over toward the front of the apartment and leaned against the black Chevy. We just stood there. Looking up at the night sky. I told him it had to be fate. We met for a reason and that reason needed to be fulfilled. He watched my lips move as I spoke, and he smiled toward me.

"Darling I do believe this was fate." He grabbed my hand and told me to look up at the stars. He told me, "look at all of them, all the millions of stars, they are here for us." I moved closer to him and held his hand tight. "Out of the millions of stars, millions of people, we found each other in such a fucked-up place, that I wasn't supposed to be in, and we showed up at the same time." I smiled toward him. "This isn't anything *but* fate." And from then on, that's what drew me toward him, that we met because we were supposed to, that it must have been fate.

He was so wonderful, the most amazing person I have ever known.

But in that moment, little did I know, it was a twisted sort of fate.

Chapter 22

Sweetheart

Bryce and I decided we were finished smoking for the night, so we called it quits, he put out the blunt and flicked it into a bush nearby. There wasn't enough left to keep it. "C'mon sweetheart lets go to bed." In this moment I realized I had to let my mom know what was happening, That I wouldn't be home for the night, and I had to think fast. At first, I thought of lying, telling her I was at Malory's house, catching up after the hospital incident. But I knew the truth would come back around to bite me in the ass sooner or later, so I just decided to tell them the truth and hope for the best.

I texted my mom and told her, "Hey mom, I'm staying at Bryce's for the night, hope you don't mind, I love you." Then I added two yellow heart emoji's next to my text and hit send.

"Whatcha up to?" Bryce questioned as I stood by the kitchen table sending a text to my mom.

"Just letting my mom know I'm not going to be home for the night." Bryce was setting up the pullout couch in the middle of the living room. I stood close by as he pulled out the bed. I set the blankets on top and situated two pillows each as he went to the kitchen to get us something to drink. He brought me back a cup of water and kissed me on the cheek. I placed the cup on the mantel and asked him for a shirt to sleep in. He handed me a big sweatshirt and I thanked him, I told him I'd be right back. I needed to get changed into the sweatshirt, so I headed toward the bathroom to get into it.

When I stepped out from the bathroom he was laying on the bed, on top of the covers. Everything still felt light, and amazing, my stomach kept dropping and I loved the feeling of being free. "Why are you not under the covers? Aren't you cold?" He just smirked and shook his head no. I could tell how calm weed made him, it does the opposite for me, all I wanted to do was talk to him.

I stepped toward the bed and sat on the edge while I checked my phone for a response from my mother "Okay, just please be safe, I love you, have a good night." I clicked the lock button and set my phone on the floor next to the bed. I laid down and rolled over to face Bryce. He was laying on his back looking up at the ceiling. As I moved closer to him and gradually moved under the covers he followed in my lead, placing the covers over himself.

"Why are you cold?" he asked.

"Freezing." He pulled me toward him and had me cuddle up next to him. He was so warm, I could tell why he didn't need a blanket, me on the other hand, my hands were like ice cubes.

"Yanno this could be a story, like you and me." He laughed at what I said. "No but like I'm serious, how we met, what we went through to get there, and how we found fate. The jokes you tell me, the cute phrases you think of, our minds work like a script." I was too high to realize if I was making any sense. "I'm sorry I'm a tad high right now you'll have to excuse my dumb remarks." He just pulled me in tighter and he said, "Write about us, that's what you do." I rolled my eyes and I don't remember much afterward, I must of fell fast asleep in his arms.

Chapter 23

Fucked up, Insecure, Neurotic, and Emotional

When I woke up in the morning, Bryce was already awake. He wasn't in the bed any longer, it was just me by myself. I slowly sat up and let the covers roll off my body, I rubbed my eyes to get the gross crust out of them and sat there looking at the television in the near distance, when we went to bed, the TV had the opening credits of the movie *"Sing"* but I guess someone turned them off because it was just a plain black screen. I heard the toilet flush then saw Bryce come out around the corner.

"Morning Darling." He said to me as he walked toward the bed. When he approached, he held up my chin and pressed his lips against my forehead to kiss me. I smiled back at him.

"Good morning," I said to him.

"How are you?" he asked me.

"I'm fine, how are you this morning?" he looked me in the eyes and shook his head. "What?" I asked him.

"You're fine?" he questioned me.

"Well I guess I'm better than fine, it was just a knee-jerk reaction."

"I hope you're not fine, Fucked up, Insecure, Neurotic, and Emotional." He looked at me pretty seriously and I laughed a little, surprised there was an acronym for the word fine. "We learnt that in Alcoholics Anonymous."

"Well I'm pretty fucked up, seeming as where we met. Ive always been insecure, not sure about being neurotic, but definitely emotional." I said to him.

"Surprised you're not an alcoholic then." I could tell he was kidding but it made me think, about how I wasn't an alcoholic but people in my life were, and that scared me. I knew how it affected my father and I knew Bryce struggled but I'd never seen him in the throes of addiction. I never wanted to see that side of him, I was proud he wanted to get better.

~

We didn't spend much more time together that day, Bryce and his brother JT had to go to work, JT owned a landscaping business, it was just starting up and he offered Bryce a job to get back on his feet again. Bryce showered, put on his camo work pants and his JT landscaping business shirt. He strapped on his work boots that now had pink laces and he was ready to work. I kiss him goodbye once he walked me to my car and I told him goodbye.

"No it's I'll see you later, goodbyes are forever remember?"

"Oh right, I forgot, I'll see you later Bryce."

"See you later Darling."

Chapter 24

Deedee

The next day I woke up to a text from Bryce telling my "Good morning beautiful." The time stamp said 7:12am and I checked the clock it was 8:30am when I had woken up. I immediately texted him back.

"Good morning, hope work treats you well today." He didn't answer right away, which I was okay with, he was busy with work, I just wanted him to know I cared about his day and his wellbeing.

That day I kept myself busy with tasks, trying not to think too much about the next time I'd see or talk to him. I didn't want to seem needy, so I made sure to let him be throughout the day.

For starters I cleaned my room. I went through my clothes and sorted out what needed to be thrown in the laundry and what was clean and could be put away. I tended to throw my clothes everywhere, clean or dirty, and thought my future self could deal with it. My future self never appreciated it, but it's not like I ever stopped mixing clothes on the floor.

I walked my laundry basket to the laundry room and opened up the washing machine. Tossed my dirty clothes in all together and spread some detergent right on tip. Growing up we never separated whites and darks, so I was accustomed to just throwing in everything together. I closed the top and let my clothes run their cycle. Then it was onto the next task.

Tidying up the rest of my disastrous room. I got a hold of all the empty water bottles from my dresser and nightstand and threw them into a plastic bag from Target. I set the bag outside of my room to deal with it later. I finished up by getting everything on my vanity and nightstand in order, just organizing everything and keeping them in one place.

Finally, my cleaning finished off with me making my bed and sweeping the floor clean. I went over to my phone which had been playing music, at that current time it was blasting *"Because of you"* by Kelly Clarkson. A true classic if you ask me.

When I checked my phone, the time shown 9:45am, I had killed about an hour cleaning my room, I scrolled through my notifications and nothing too interesting was happening in the world of social media, just random twitter posts and someone liking my picture on Instagram from a while ago, which I always found a tad weird, but appreciated the like.

I set my phone on my bed and took out a lighter from my dresser and lit a candle from Bath and Body Works, the scent was Japanese cherry blossom, it had always been my favorite. I walked over to my just made bed and once again, wrecked it by getting under the covers and taking a nap. As I was dosing off I was wondering about how when people meet they never expect to be where they end up. Like Bryce and I, I bet he never thought that we'd end up together and I sure as hell never thought of it that way. He just seemed like a nice guy to connect with in Overbrooke, but things change, and we happened to work out.

I cuddled up next to my Deedee (that's what I called my baby blanket ever since I was little, and yes, I still had my baby blanket at eighteen years old). I fell right to sleep.

Chapter 25

Slipping

I woke up again from my nap around 5:00pm, I had been asleep for quite a while, I didn't sleep too well the night before so that must have explained why I slept so soundly during the day. I woke up to no messages from Bryce, worried a little that he hadn't texted me, I called him... no answer. I set my phone down and got out of bed, and decided to take a hot shower to calm my nerves.

In the shower I think about the past few days and how well Bryce and I were getting along, worried that soon enough it would probably end, like most things do.

Hopping out of the shower I throw my hair into a towel and brush my teeth, wiping away the fog on the mirror to display a distorted version of myself. I laugh a little and spit the toothpaste out of my mouth. I brush my hair out of its tangled mess and throw it up into a messy bun (I've always hated doing my hair, there was just too much of it). Walking back to my room I slip on some leggings and a sweatshirt, comfy attire is always necessary when needing to go on a mission, yes I said mission.

This is when I decided I would surprise Bryce back at his house. Mission in full awareness I grab my keys and set out for the road. The drive there is not a quick one so I had ample time to listen to some music and calm my nerves. I decided to stop at Wawa on the way there, grab him some food since I knew he'd be hungry after work. I orders two subs and got us some soda. I was hoping he'd like what I picked for him.

Approaching the house I pull up right to the door and notice no cars were in the driveway. Confused I sat there for a beat, looking around waiting for cars to appear. "Are they not home?" questioning as I sit in my car. I decide to go up to the door anyway, subs in hand, drinks in the other I walk up and ring the doorbell... waiting for a moment and realizing there was no answer. I rang again... waited and felt defeated. I looked around e realizing how dark it had gotten. I thought maybe I should call Bryce, see if he'd answer this time. I set my bags down, took a seat on the curb and dialed his number waiting for the ring, it rang again and again until I got sent to voicemail. I got up confused and panicked and tried the door handle, low and behold the door swung open displaying the stairs in front of me. I grabbed my bags and thought, mine as well go in. (In hindsight this was sort of breaking and entering but at this point my mind was a mess and I was worried about everyone and where they were). I make my way up the stairs and peer over to my right exposing the living room and realize there Bryce was... passed out on the couch. A sigh of relief came over my body and a smile appeared wider than imaginable. The lights were off, but the television was still running.

I walk passed Bryce and set my things on the kitchen table. As I turned around to walk over to Bryce I noticed a bottle on the table. My heart sank, realizing what this meant. I walked over to the lairds bottle and picked it up, empty. A whole handle gone. I go to the kitchen to throw out his mess when I found multiple bottles of different vodka, different shapes and sizes, all empty or barley showing any evidence.

I started to well up, like the water that was held in my body could expel through my eyes like waterfalls. I know I felt defeated, but what must Bryce feel? He just went through all this treatment to end up right back where he was again.

I approached Bryce as calmly in my mannerisms as I could. I wanted to scream at him I wanted to show him how insane this was, but I knew that wasn't justified and I knew that wouldn't change what had happened anyway. I said his name a few time, then tried to shake him to wake up, no answer either times. I sat down next to his curled up legs and thought about him. I just sat there, going through this whirlwind of emotions. Thinking what have I got myself into… stressed and defeated I got up, no longer any appetite to eat my sub I set them in the fridge.

I found a piece of paper and a pen and wrote him a letter:
"Dear Bryce,
I found you tonight, laying on the couch, consumed by bottles a plenty of vodka. I don't know what to say, I don't know how to feel. I don't understand what you're going through, but I can promise you i'm not leaving your side, you told me If this ever happened to run, to run and never look back, but I cant. My heart is filled with emotions I can't explain, and their all for you. I don't know what else to say besides I love you.
Signed, Reese"

I set the not next to him on the table. Grabbed my bag and keys and headed out, locking the door behind me, since last time no one thought to do that.

Chapter 26

I Love You

I woke up the next morning to a missed call from Bryce, No voicemail though. I didn't want to answer him, because at this point I was scared about his response to my letter. I thought about writing how I loved him and I regretted the decision. Not because I didn't mean it, but because I was afraid he either wouldn't say it back, or completely avoid the gesture. Before answering him I decided to take a shower, fix myself, and put something in my stomach. I realized I never ate dinner the night before and it was probably still sitting in his fridge.

After feeling like more of myself I decided to call Bryce, confront the situation head on, full speed ahead! I dialed his number and it rang a few beats before he answered.

"What's up darling?" my heart stopped, his voices was raspy and alcohol ridden I could feel it in my bones.

"Hey Bryce, just showered and got ready for the day, not much is going on." It was weird this started off as such a normal conversation... I was excepted it to be more intense, maybe he would bring up me breaking into his house to start... but I guess that wasn't the first thing on his mind.

"That's good" there was a pause, he didn't have anything else to say. I waited to respond, choosing my words carefully before I blurted out something dumb.

"How was your morning" in reality I wanted to be snarky and ask how his night went but what good would that do?

"It was hectic, kids running around and screaming, JT and his fiancé bickering, I just sat there, drank my coffee and let the commotion commence."

"That sounds like a handful haha" my laugh trailed off and I could feel myself whelming up for tears, I tend to be an emotional person if you haven't noticed. I couldn't help but think what had happened so terrible last night that drove him to drink.

"Yeah I need to get out of this place as soon as possible" was him living with JT and the kids driving him to drink? Am I just trying to think of any possible reason to the catastrophe that was last night.
There was a moment of silence in between our thoughts. We both didn't know how to react or speak to each other, we both know what happened but neither of us wanted to speak about it.

"So, you stopped by last night" FINALLY.

"Yeah I did" short and simple.

"How did you get in?" uh oh...

"The door was unlocked so I walked in, I was worried about everyone" perfect answer if I don't say so myself.

"Gotcha, so..." his "so" trailed on while my thoughts ran rapid with what to say next.

"So..." I didn't know how to respond.

"Did you bring over subs?" THAT WAS HIS RESPONSE

"Yeah I was hungry, thought you might be too."

"I ate one this morning it was great, thank you."

"Yeah I lost my appetite last night" BALLSY.

"Yeah? Why's that?" a quick response.

"I saw some things I probably wasn't supposed to see."

"And what might that be?" I paused, thinking of the right choice of words.

"Some empty bottles"
Silence.

He didn't respond, he stopped in his tracks. I didn't think this would catch him off guard, by my letter he knew I was there and he knew what I saw, he saw it too.

"Bryce?" I was worried with the two minute silence that was lingering.

"Yeah?" THAT'S IT?!

"Yeah… you didn't answer your making me worried"

"Just thinking about that letter you wrote" oh here it goes. "You said something funny"

"Funny? What was funny about it?"

"I love you" HE SAID IT. Well he repeated what I said… but he said it !!

"That's funny?"

"Well, not funny it's ironic" Ironic? "Because Reese" a pause. "It just so happens, I love you too."

"Bryce… don't mess with me" my heart was racing faster than a horse with a whip.

"I would never mess with you."

"I don't know what to say to be honest."

"Just say see you later and I'll talk to you soon."

"See you later Bryce" and I clicked the end button.

Chapter 27

Glazed Eyes

I woke up the next morning with all thoughts of Bryce, everything that happened and what this would mean for our future together. After tossing my messy hair up into a bun and rolling out of bed I took the longest sip of water you could imagine, I was very parched. I set the empty bottle down and turned toward my phone to see if anyone had messaged me. One message from Bryce appeared on my phone, "Good morning beautiful, i'm headed off to work and ill text you when I have the chance, I'd love for you to come visit me today." A smile a mile long stretched across my face, him saying i'm beautiful, him telling me to visit him, all made my heart flutter with excitement.

I texted him back, "Good Morning handsome! I just got out of bed, I'd love to see you today, just let me know when you're free" I set my phone down and went to the kitchen to make some breakfast. My mom was there, watching the news and drinking her morning coffee (which is not sweet enough by the way). I made myself a very light and sweet cup of coffee and poured some frosted flakes in a huge bowl, while I was letting it sink into the milk to get soggy (that's how I like it) I said good morning to my mom and we talked for a little. She asked how Bryce was doing and how we were getting along. I paused, wanted to tell her about his relapse but knowing if I did she'd have something not so great to say about it, so I left it be and made sure to push that to the side. "He's great! He's so sweet to me and the way he interacts with his nieces is precious! We get along really well, no bumps in the road yet!" Made up a little lie, but one white lie never hurt anybody, right? She congratulated me on the swell relationship and she walked away to hop in the shower. Alone at last, just how I like it to be in my morning routine, just me, a cup of coffee, and some soggy frosted flakes! I pulled out my journal to write an entry about Bryce, I wanted to process the situation of relapse, I wanted to put it down on paper and forget it ever happened (if that was even possible). After writing my entry I wrote some poetry, here's an excerpt:

> "His eyes like glass
> glazed with the ambition of an athlete
> but the leaking soul of a poet
> his sorrows drowned with a bottle
> and my heart filled with pain."

Just something to calm my soul and get the words out in my own way.

After my bowl was stained dry I put my bowl in the sink and headed back to my room, checking my phone for messages from Bryce.
He had texted me "Come see me whenever! You can pick me up from this job site if you'd like, JT left and he said he wasn't coming back to finish the work, he had some business to get done, whatever that means." Confused on what JT could possibly skip work for and leave his brother without a ride home is beyond me. Annoyed with JT I decided I'd go visit Bryce and pick him up from the job site.

"Send me the address! I can leave in 20."

Chapter 28

Paid

When I arrived at the site I realized it was just someone's house, not sure why I thought any different. I texted Bryce I had arrived and he told me he'd come get me. The back gate swung open and there he was in all his handsome glory, his hat on backward, his camo shorts and work boots all stained with dirt and mud. He motioned for me to come over, I took the keys out of the ignition and stated my way over to him. When I saw him I couldn't help but jump into his arms, he wrapped his work hands around me and laid a huge kiss on my forehead. "What's up Darling?" I smiled.

"Not much just excited to see you!" He had me follow him into the back where he was doing his work, he was adding gravel and rocks to the outside of this guy's pool, it was a beautiful house and a beautiful backyard I couldn't help but stare at all its glory.

"Pretty nice huh?" He said to me.

"Way more than nice, its beautiful."

"Well when you have to stare at is while doing his dirty work it becomes kind of daunting." I could only imagine. "Well my work here is done today, let's get out of here, maybe hit a diner?" I smiled and shook my head yes, and we were on our way out.

~

When we got back to Jamestown we decided to go to a local diner by his house and grab a bite to eat. I asked him if he wanted to change first and his response was "I need to show these people im a working man".

So we sat in a booth in a retro looking diner and ordered some food, I got chicken fingers per usual and he got a corned beef sandwich on rye with extra mayo. He looked me in my eyes and smirked "Reese" he said I nudged my head for him to continue, "You have the most stunning eyes, I could stare into them all day if I could" I laughed, never getting such a remark like that before turned my head.

"Oh stop it, they're not that great."

"To me, they are." I just smiled back at him and changed the subject.

"How was work? And what happened with JT?"

"It was work, shoveling rocks isn't the most exciting thing. He told me someone else offered him a paying job at their house so he went to do that, supposedly…" He trailed off his words and looked around him as if he was uncomfortable with the conversation.

"Supposedly?" I responded

"Samantha is worried he's using again." My heart sank, I knew he had a history of heroin and that's the scariest thing to have taken ahold of you.

"So what do you think of that?"

"I think she's probably right, hes been acting super weird lately."

Our food came to the table and that was the end of that conversation. I didn't want to pry and I didn't want to make it seem like I was putting myself in a position where I don't belong. I ate my nuggets and he ate his sandwich pretty much in silence. I guess we were both thinking about JT. I was mostly thinking about Josie and Hayden and what that meant for them. They don't deserve to grow up in a household of drugs and alcohol and by the looks of it that exactly what was happening between JT and Bryce. I know what it's like to be surrounded by that. Not heroin but cocaine and bottle of booze, for sure and that broke my heart.

At the end of our meal Bryce looked at me concerned and I asked him what was wrong.

"I forgot to tell you." My heart sank.

"What?" confused as to what he would say next.

"JT hasn't paid me yet for the work ive done with him." Relieved that it wasn't anything more extreme I smiled and told him I had it covered. He stood up and came around to my side of the booth and gave me a kiss on the forehead thanking me for the meal.

All of a sudden his phone starts to ring and he took it out of his pocket, it was from an unknown number. He didn't answer and I didn't ask anything of it.

Chapter 29

Disbelief

When we got back in the car he instantly held my hand and told me how much I meant to him. "Reese, I really do appreciate you and all your beauty, you make wanting to live a lot easier." I could've cried at how sweet his comment was, but instead I planted a kiss on him and told him not to worry about a thing. "Reese?"

"Yes, Bryce?" I questioned.

"I have a favor to ask you, and I understand if you say no but you have to understand the importance of this task."

"Continue…" I said with question in my tone.

"I need a bottle of vodka, and no I don't want it to get drunk, I can't just abruptly stop drinking or I could go through withdrawal and die. I need it to wean myself off of it." I stopped for a moment and thought about the consequences of me saying yes or me saying no. I thought about if I said yes what if i'm just giving into his addiction… but, on the flipside if I say no will he really go through a bad withdrawal and possibly die…

"Bryce, I don't know if that's the best idea."

"Reese you don't understand I need it to survive." He said very strongly in his tone.

"I'm scared to give in and let you have your poison, what if you can't stop yourself."

"I will and I can i've done it before I just need you to trust me." I sat and didn't say anything terrified of either of my choices I stayed silent instead. "REESE!" this was the first time he had raised his voice at me and it startled me. I turned to him in disbelief.

"I need a fucking bottle or i'm going to die, do you want me to die? It'll be on your hands if someone wakes up and finds me dead." Still in disbelief with how he was talking to me I turned the car on with no words from my mouth and began to drive to the liquor store, I guess I was giving in, and I didn't want to. But I was afraid I would lose him if I didn't, to either him dying or cutting me off for not being by his side and helping him.

"Where the fuck are you going?"

"To the liquor store."

Chapter 30

Mixed Feelings

After the liquor store and dropping him off I had a long ride home with just me and my thoughts. We didn't even speak after the last interaction we had, he got out of the car, slammed the door and didn't even say goodbye, even after me buying him liquor. I had no words, just a lot of mixed feelings. How could he yell at me like that? And make me feel like his addiction would be in my hands if I didn't buy him a bottle of Lairds. I was disgusted and heartbroken, not only with him but myself.

After seeing my father day in and day out drinking into oblivion you would think I'd have a stronger backbone to say no, but alas. After being accused of wanted someone dead, your emotions just run rapid, they go off the handle and I went into pilot mode. I didn't want to lose him so I did what was best for our relationship. Or so I thought…

~

This was Bryce and I's start to rock bottom. Our eternal race between love and hate. Fate had brought us together, but at what cost? The rest of this novel with consist of my telling of the horrendous episodes that has followed Bryce and I, and our battle with his addiction and my persistence.

Chapter 31

Drunk

After our first fight thing started to dwindle. The lovey dovey person that Bryce was shortly faded once I sparked a fire in him. I missed the person he used to be, and tried for dear life to hold onto something that was already gone. I went over the next day to surprise him and visit him. He wasn't so excited to see me.

"Why are you here?"

"Bryce why are you acting this way? Can't we just talk?"

"You should leave." I paused looking him in his eyes trying to read them as they moved back and forth.

"Why?"

"Because you don't need to see me like this."

"Like what? Drunk? It's nothing I haven't seen before trust me."

"GO! LEAVE ME ALONE!"

So I left, I wasn't going to pry and I wasn't going to beg.

Chapter 32

Carly

A few days later I received a call from Bryce, he left a voice message since I was working at the time. "What's up Reese, I miss you, please call me back when you get this." I was shocked to have received that message. It felt like the old Bryce was back, maybe he kicked his habit again. When I got off of work I called him back, he instantly answered. "What's up darling?".

"Nothing much Bryce, Just got out of work, how've you been?"

"Ahh Yanno living the dream, battling this alcohol but im doing better, other than my living situation."

"What happened to staying with JT and Samantha?"

"It was a mix between me getting kicked out for fighting with JT about his drug use and me wanting to leave the environment because of his drug use, so basically drugs."

"Where are you staying now?"

"Currently at my old sponsor's house, he said I could stay as long as I'd like."

"Well i'm glad you're in an alcohol free space."

"Do you want to see me?" of course I did, I missed him so much.

"Of course I do."

"Come by my sponsor's house, I'll give you the address we can watch movies and eat some food."

"Once you send it I'll be on my way, See you later."

~

I arrived at the house he sent me and I walked up the gravel driveway to expose the front door, I knocked and waited. A big bald guy walked to the door and opened the screen in front of me "Well Welcome! You must be Reese, i've heard so much about you!" I smiled and walked inside

"Hey, it's so nice to meet you i'm sorry what's your name?"

"Charlie's the name!" he was a very joyful man, and I loved that about him, I wish I could have the enthusiasm he had all the time. "Come on in, Bryce is just getting out of the shower and he'll meet us in the living room." I sat down on the couch in front of a ton of book cases, there was over 500 books, no joke his whole place was filled with them.

"So, you like to read huh?" I asked him to spark his interest.

"Oh man do I love to read, I like mostly horror, Stephen King is my favorite."

"I love to read too! I have to be honest though i've never dove into the horror, i'm interested in it though, maybe you can give me some recommendations."

"Oh boy I'd love to! I actually think we're going to watch the new *IT*" if that's okay with you."
"Sounds great to me!"

Bryce walked out and I could smell his shampoo as he walked to the kitchen. "Want some vodka?" he said to me and I stopped looked at Charlie and didn't know what to say. "It's a joke Reese, you can laugh" I laughed quite sparingly.

Charlie commented "Can you not scare our guest away? She just got here."

"You're right, i'm sorry Reese just thought the room needed a little laughter."

I responded, "No, no it was funny, just caught me off guard for a second." Then his phone started to ring, he looked at his phone and quickly looked up at me.

"I have to take this." He went into the next room and took his phone call, the walls are paper thin so I could hear everything that was said from his end. Including, "Im not with another girl, I love you Carly". I could feel my stomach rumble and my heart fall to my feet. Who is Carly?

I've never heard of a Carly, but maybe she knows me? Since hes referring to having no one else over. Charlie was in his room at this point, doing whatever Charlies do I guess. I stood up with tears in my eyes and I was ready to scream. I paced around the living room for a bit and decided to leave, I walked outside and was about to get in my car when Bryce stepped out. Where are you going?

"Maybe you can invite Carly over since you love her so much." He stopped in his tracks, you could see the gears turning inside of his head. In that moment you could feel how stupid he felt.

"What the fuck are you talking about?" he wanted me to feel crazy, thinking I heard something I didn't.

"Bryce i'm not dumb, and I know what I heard"

"Fine, leave, I don't care about you."

And so I left.

Chapter 33

ER

Bryce and I hadn't talked for a few days but I was giving him space, after our last interaction I didn't know what to say to him anyway. I was stocking the shelves at Journey's shoe store, getting the stock room ready for audit. And that's when I received a call, from Bryce. He was crying and freaking out to me, apologizing and telling me he needs me. I heard that he was in a car so I told him to slow down and breathe and I asked where he was. "I'm in the car with Jenny". Jenny's his life-long friend and used to be girlfriend years ago.

"Okay where are you going?"

Under his muffled tears I heard him saying over and over "I'm sorry". With no response to where he was going, I told him to put Jenny on the phone. "Hello?" this is the first time I heard her voice.

"Where are you guys going?"

"We're on our way to the hospital, Bryce needs help." My heart sank, the bottle of booze I got him slipped him right back to where he was. "Did you buy him a bottle of vodka?"

"I did, and i'm so sorry I didn't know what else to do he was yelling at me that he was going to die."

"I'm not blaming you I just didn't know if what he said was true, he likes to lie about things." She stopped talking for a moment then said "If you could come to the hospital…he really wants to see you before he's admitted".

I checked the time and I was off in 20 minutes. "I get off the clock in 20 minutes I can meet you there after work".

"That's perfect, he wants to go to Brick hospital and we're just leaving Jamestown."

"See you soon." And I ended the call. Not knowing what truly just happened and not being able to process the situation I left work early, told my boss I had some family emergency that I needed to tend to, and I was on the road to the hospital.

~

Arriving at the hospital felt like I was being admitted to the psych ward once again, bringing back the memories of intake and the whole entire process; as I was waiting there for them I couldn't stop thinking about how good we were in the beginning.

Jenny texted me that they arrived and were waiting in front of the emergency room. I got out of my car hesitant and walked to where they were standing. Bryce was a lot more calm than he was on the phone, but I could tell his demeanor was off. I introduced myself to Jenny and then said hello to Bryce. Bryce just leaned in and gave me the biggest hug of my life. I'm sorry, I'm so sorry. I'm sorry about relapsing and I'm sorry about Carly, she's gone, she's out of the picture I told her my heart is with you, and I promise you it is, if it wasn't I wouldn't have called you. And for some reason I bought it. I took his words to heart and believed him.

"Okay Bryce, okay, I believe you." He kissed me and then we walked into the ER. All three of us sat and waited in silence till his name was called. We all had one big group hug and we sent him off.

Chapter 34

Green light

The next big event in our relationship is a dark one, so prepare yourself. We had fought day in and day out. It felt like the fate that brought us together was diminishing and the hope I had for our relationship was significantly fading. What once felt like a fairytale was now a trapped vortex of hate.

We had been going at each other's necks all day, constantly bickering. On our ride back to the motel he was staying at we had a rough patch. When I picked him up from Walmart my phone was sitting in the center console, untouched and un to known our next big demise.
As he got in the car he was already mad I was a little later than I said I'd be, I needed gas, what did he want form me? I was driving him everywhere he should've been grateful, but alas.

My phone lit up with a buzz, it was a snapchat notification. Leaving it untouched while I was driving, Bryce picked it up. I didn't see the phone and I had no idea what it was at the time. He said instantly "Pull the fuck over". Confused and unknowing I questioned why. "Who is tom?!" he said with a sternness in his voice.

"What are you talking about" I asked.

"Tom, from snapchat" it clicked in my brain and I realized it was one of my friends from school.

"Oh, no worries he's a friend from school."

"PULL THE FUCK OVER NOW." At this point I was scared and concerned for our safety so I pulled back into the parking lot of Walmart and asked him to please calm down. "why do you have boys in your phone messaging you?"

"Bryce, I told you, he was a friend from high school... I haven't talked to him since I graduated he's probably just checking in on me."

"No man should be checking up on you, if it's not me it's not necessary" scared it would start a fight I responded quickly

"Bryce ill delete him, it's no big deal" I took my phone back and blocked his snapchat. "See, he's blocked it's all good now".

"Blocked? I want him deleted, I know how snapchat works you can go and unblock him at any time." Panicked I responded,

"Okay, okay, ill figure out how to do it later can we just go back to the motel now?" he was quiet for a second and I started the car back up and pulled out. Halfway there it was completely silent, neither of us spoke a word until Bryce of course spoke up.

"You're just a whore you know that?" I was setback with this comment, I hadn't done anything wrong Bryce just assumes and runs with his imagination.

"Bryce can you please stop, I didn't do anything!"

"YOURE TALKING TO OTHER MEN". At this point I wasn't going to be screamed at while driving so I pulled the car over to the side of the road.

"I'm pulling over to talk about this because I can't drive and be distracted" trying to stay as calm as possible while being screamed at is not an easy task.

"Why the fuck do you have other men in your phone?"
I couldn't keep my cool any longer, "FOR THR LAST TIME, HE WAS A FRIEND." This was the worst choice I could make, and I regret it looking back.

"Don't you DARE scream at me like that" a hand swung toward my head and I dodged it with a swift jerk to the left. He had never gotten physical with me, and this was the last time I ever wanted to be in that position. Shaken and scared I started to cry, small droplets of tears fell from my eyes as I started the ignition again and drove onto the street. I didn't have anything to say, I just wanted to get him out of my car as quick as possible.

"Oh so now you can't speak? You raise your voice and now you can't speak?" I was sick and tired of being beaten down and battered for things I couldn't control. "You scared now? Huh?" still in silence I muffled my cries, praying hoping to the god above to come and save me. I used to think he was my fate but in that moment I realized all I needed was my faith.

"You're a fucking whore, a cheating hoe."

I was so done with it all.

I wanted it to stop.

I needed him to stop.

And in that moment I felt just as low as when I was admitted to the hospital. I was stuck.

We hit a red light and I stopped. But when it turned green I didn't go, I froze. Everything in my body was shutting down, I was over everything again. With my foot on the brake Bryce says "Are you stupid the light is green, go!" I quickly put the car in park and jumped out of the car. I ran full speed ahead to the other side of oncoming traffic, wanting someone to take me away. Wanting my god to swift me off my feet and bring me with him to the glory that is above.

Bryce ran out behind me, running toward me he grabs me and pushed me onto the grass before the car that was approaching could bring me to my demise.

I laid there, silent, with dried tears staining my face I was just still.

"REESE."

No response.

"please baby answer me"

He called me baby again.

I finally responded after what felt like an eternity, "Im so done Bryce, i'm so over it."

Bryce responded, "Darling, i'm so sorry, I was acting insane, you're none of the things I said, let's just forget about it please".

I got up with no words running from my mouth, he helped me back to the car and put me in the passenger seat. He drove the rest of the way back to the motel in complete silence.

When we arrived I jumped back into the driver's seat, he apologized a few more time and kissed me. And that was the end of our night together.

Chapter 35

Voicemails

Each time Bryce and I got together it was an experience for a movie, there was always something happening to make it seem like a bad flick. This time I had my first run in with the police.

Bryce needed to fix his truck and I was the only one there to help him and of course, I stuck by his side. At this point he had been staying with me and my parents. I drove him to his truck to get it back up and running so he could get to work on his own (not legally, he didn't have a license because of his DUI's).

When we arrived it was about 8:00pm, too dark to do work on a car with no light. Before we attempted to prop my car as a light source he went up to Samantha and JT's apartment for something, I didn't see what went down as I was still in my car. When he came back he instructed me to move my car so the headlights were facing his truck, I tried my best but apparently that wasn't good enough, he screamed at me, telling me I didn't know what I was doing. He told me to get out and that he would do it. As he hopped in the front seat three cop cars pulled up behind us blinding us with their headlights. Over the loud speaker the officer instructed us both to get out of the car with our hands up. I did as I was told. My heart inside of my stomach I wondered what was going on. I has never been in this type of situation. What do you do when a cop pulls up other than listen to their instructions?

An officer took Bryce to one side of the driveway and another took me to the opposite. I has shaking, I couldn't feel my legs because of how scared I was. My palms could have filled a river with sweat, I was astonished at what was happening. The officer didn't say a word to me at first, we just watched as Bryce was taking a sobriety test, and he was epically failing, he couldn't even walk in a straight line, it was an absolute mess. They told him to say the ABC's which was a complete mess, his words slurred together and he could barely finish. The officers searched the car and found a water bottle apparently filled with vodka that I wasn't even aware was in there. They searched some more and I saw them pull out a small plastic bag, of what I assumed was weed. The officer I was with asked me if I knew about what was in the car and honestly I didn't.

"I'm so sorry, I honestly had no idea."

"Honey, what are you doing with a man like him?"

I stood there silent not knowing how to respond. What was I doing with a man like this? I guess my love for the person I fell for was pulling me through it all. She cuffed me and walked me to a cop car as the other officer did the same to Bryce. As soon as the cop car that held Bryce drove away the lady officer came around back and uncuffed me.

"I know this wasn't you're doing and this isn't your fault, you're not in trouble but im going to bring you to the station."

We drove up the street to the police station and I called my mom to tell her what happened, they were impounding my car so she had to come pick me up. She was furious, upset, and confused. As any mother should be. I begged for her to bail Bryce out but she wouldn't, I had to leave him there overnight.

~

The next morning I woke up to a multitude of voicemails from Bryce. "You're just a pathetic 18 year old, how fucking dare you leave me in a cell." Another one "You're a piece of shit human for doing this to me" to be honest the voicemails were barely audible he was so drunk. That was the end of seeing Bryce for a while.

Chapter 36

Losing Feeling

After the interaction with the police I didn't have contact with Bryce for a while, so I had time to focus on myself and my job. I just recently received a position at Red Robin as a hostess, a job I wasn't familiar with but excited to get started.

As my shifts went on I met some amazing co-workers, one of them named Nicholas, he was one of the line cooks and he quickly became a good friend of mine. One day after work he invited me over to hangout as his place and watch movies, and have a beer or two (I know I wasn't old enough but he was and it felt safe). I decided to say yes and expand our friendship. Since I wasn't over the idea of Bryce and Nicolas had a girlfriend our relationship was strictly platonic. I had no strong feelings for him other than our strong friendship bond. He knew about Bryce and what I had gone through with him, he understood and listened which is really all I could ask for in a friend.

Upon arrival his house was beautiful, with a light baby blue exterior with a glorious white door, I felt like I was in a movie. I knocked on the door and was greeted with Nicholas and two small puppies. They were so friendly and welcoming which made me feel even more comfortable being there. Immediately Nicholas asked me if I wanted a beer, I accepted and we sat on the couch. It was silent, we weren't really talking and I felt slightly awkward. I had never felt like this around him so I was confused. There was no television in his living room so he asked if I wanted to go to the bedroom to watch a movie, slightly uncomfortable I reluctantly said yes. I didn't want to be rude and I thought I was just feeling weird for no reason. I babied my drink, taking small sips. I didn't drink often and with the history of my father I wasn't the biggest fan of drinking, I guess I did it to feel included. Instead of playing a movie he just turned on the television and flipped through channels. I was watching as the channels flipped and started to feel awkwardly wrong. I felt tired, nauseas and dizzy. I started to lose feeling of my senses and couldn't feel my hand or feet, I started to panic. I looked at Nicholas with a fuzziness in my eyes, they felt dry and empty I said "I don't feel good" and that's the last thing I remember before the darkness hit. In an instant my eyes went black and my hearing was lost, and then I was completely passed out.

When I woke up from what felt like the longest nap of my life there was Nicholas on top of me and felt no clothes on my bottom half. I screamed, it was the only reaction I could think to portray, he held my mouth shut and looked me dead in the eyes, said nothing, just stared. I wiggled and struggled until my saving grace came. A phone call. Nicholas's phone started to ring in the next room, he got off of me and sprinted toward his phone. I quickly got up, losing my balance and still not being able to feel most of my body I struggled to get my jeans on, but I accomplished my mission. Grabbed my keys and ran out of the house all the way to my car, locking the doors instantly and starting the ignition as fast as possible I drove off with the fear of him following me.

I reported the incident but the officers didn't believe me, so that was the end of faith in the justice system for me.

Chapter 37

I am Free

Bryce and I had been on and off for about three months. It was a long three months of bickering, and putting up with his manipulative language. He loved to bring up the incident with the police and say I should be lucky he took the blame for the alcohol and the weed since it was in my car; but it was blatantly obvious I wasn't the one intoxicated. This comment always made my blood boil and we would constantly fight over it. The three months included him cheating on me and me running back every time.

I was stuck on the person he was when I met him in the hospital and I constantly thought maybe one day he'd be sober again, and I wanted to stick around for the Bryce I knew at first.
But, this is the part of the story how our relationship ended up in smoke and flames...

Bryce and I reconnected after two weeks of no communication, he reached out to me saying he was back staying with Charlie (his old sponsor) and he was now sober again. Giving him the benefit of the doubt I reached back out and told him how happy I was to know he was doing better. He asked me to catch a movie with him and catch up on our lives, I agreed.

I went to pick him up and when I saw him again my heart fluttered with excitement, I was excited to see a sober Bryce, the Bryce I first met, the Bryce I fell for months prior. On our way to the movie we had amazing conversation, he told me how AA was doing and how he actually ran a group recently. I was so proud of him and his treatment and couldn't wait to see where the future went from here.

~

When the movie was over we walked back to the car, as I was about to open my door I realized I didn't have my phone, I panicked. Looked at Bryce and told him I needed to go back. I went back into the theater and found my phone laying on the ground next to our seats. I picked it up and was on my way back to my car. As I was approaching the car I realized Bryce had my glove compartment open and a piece of paper in his hands, he was adamantly reading it. My heart started to race and I realized what he was holding, it was my police statement to the officers about my assault. I hadn't told Bryce about the assault because I didn't know how he'd react. I wasn't going to hide if from him forever; I just needed to find the right time to tell him and I didn't think the first day we reconnected would be the perfect time to do so. As I approached the car I opened the door slow and steady. Upon entering the car he just shows me the paper with a stern look on his face. "What is this?" he questioned.

"Bryce I can explain!" I exclaimed.

"Explain that you were hanging out with other men?" I was taken back, it wasn't like that…it was never supposed to be like that, I just got trapped in a freak accident.

"Bryce I swear I will explain it to you, It's not what you think, I wasn't there to date this man, we were just friends from work and it took a terrible turn, I was drugged!" he wasn't having my explanation.

"So you hung out with another man and were doing drugs." He misunderstood.

"Not drugs, he gave me a beer, I think it was drugged."

"EVEN WORSE, you were drinking when you know the consequences of alcohol" I didn't even think he'd react that way about it.

"Bryce I'm sorry, I regret everything that happened and I wish I could go back and change it, but it's in the past now."

"Bring me home" but I couldn't, I had therapy.

"Bryce I told you I need to go to therapy, you said you'd stay in the car while I went."

"Bring me to the mall, I'd rather walk all this shit off then ponder in your car." So that's what I did, I brought him to the mall and went to therapy.

I told my therapist about the situation and how Bryce was in my life again, I could feel the disappointment in her body language, but she would never batter me about my decisions just instruct me on the consequences of them.

~

After my therapy session I went to the mall to pick up Bryce. When I got in my car I realized I had multiple voicemails from him screaming at me: "REESE YOURE A FUCKING TERRIBLE PERSON, HOW COULD YOU DO THIS TO ME? HOW COULD YOU HURT ME LIKE THIS?" and that wasn't the end of it, there were many more calling me a hoe and a slut and stating that if I was never with a guy this wouldn't have happened.

When I arrived at the mall it was dark and raining, proper weather for the way I was feeling, I was already upset and torn down from his words I didn't even want to see him. He didn't even enter the car when I pulled up he just opened the door and stared at me.
Silence for a moment then I said "what, are you going to get in?" in a slightly snarky way, I couldn't help it, I had enough of his battering words.

"Oh so now you want me in your life? What about the other guy? Was it even true? Was it a cover-up so I wouldn't think you were cheating on me?"

"Bryce, we weren't together even if I hung out with a guy like that, it wouldn't have been cheating."

"So, you admit it!? You were seeing him for sex" which was absurd and hurtful, he was just supposed to be a friend. Someone I thought I could trust, but alas.

"I'm not admitting anything! I'm just saying!"

"Yanno what Reese, you're a whore, you're a terrible person, you deserve what happened to you and I hope all I believe in that it happens to you again."

In that moment I froze. My heart racing with hate, my body shaking with anxiety and my eyes filling with tears. I wiped my eyes and screamed at him "IM DONE." I could feel all the tension in my body, my mind wouldn't stop going in circles with all the hatred I had for him, all the questions I asked myself about if it was my fault that happened to me and the question as to why I kept going back to Bryce. In an instant I looked straight ahead to a tree, I looked back at Bryce then front again, and in that moment I wanted it to all end. I pressed the gas with the tree in full vision. Blank. My mind was blank. My eyes went blank. My heart went blank. I felt nothing and everything all in one moment. My life flashing before my eyes my head hit the steering wheel and my body like jelly with the motion of my car hitting the tree.

When my mind regained stamina I looked out my rearview mirror and saw Bryce running, not toward the car to see if I was okay, but away from the wreckage. In that moment I realized our fate had ended. Our relationship was done, in ruins more than ever. But I also realized I was free. I was one step closer to my own life's fate and no longer tied to his. I was free.

PLEASE REVIEW!

All independent authors depend upon reviews left on Amazon.com by readers to help promote their books. Without these reviews, they will hardly get any notice. Please take the time to leave a short review. Simply go to Amazon.com, find the book and go to the book's page. Under the author's name will be a list of reviews and stars. Click here and there will be a big button saying "Create your own review".
Please click here and review.

It only takes a minute

Made in the USA
Middletown, DE
17 March 2022

62799810R00080